Strong Waters

A Simple Guide to Making Beer, Wine, Cider and Other Spirited Beverages at Home

Scott Mansfield

When making a batch of wine, be sure to carbonate a few bottles. Cherry and pomegranate make excellent sparkling wines. *(Cherry Wine, page 68; Pomegranate Wine, page 79)*

You don't need a wine press to extract juice from fruit; a colander often works just as well. *("Racking," pages 45–46)*

Experiment with different types of sugar, such as the Mexican piloncillo shown here, to tailor the recipes in this book to your taste. *("Sugars," page 23)*

Hard cider is simple to make from apple or other juices. *(Basic Hard Cider, page 152)*

Strawberries make a gorgeous dry summer rosé or Strawberry Melomel *(page 142)*.

Blackberries and honey form the base of this smooth and luscious melomel.
Serve it as you would a red wine. *(Blackberry Melomel, page 140)*

Elderberries were traditionally thought to protect against both illness and bad luck. You can use fresh or dried fruits to make a hearty, port-like wine. *(Elderberry Wine, page 76)*

Made with roses and honey, rhodomel is an exotic and aromatic beverage to drink on special occasions. *(Rhodomel, page 136)*

An eighteenth-century Scottish duke is credited with creating the rich and delicious Atholl Brose, an after-dinner liquor made from whisky, cream, honey, and oats.
(Atholl Brose, page 201)

THE EXPERIMENT

BECAUSE EVERY BOOK IS A TEST OF NEW IDEAS

Strong Waters

A Simple Guide to Making Beer, Wine, Cider
and Other Spirited Beverages at Home

■

Scott Mansfield

Foreword by Anya Fernald

THE EXPERIMENT

NEW YORK

The Experiment, LLC
260 Fifth Avenue
New York, NY 10001–6425
www.theexperimentpublishing.com

Many of the designations used by manufacturers and sellers to distinguish their products are claimed as trademarks. Where those designations appear in this book and The Experiment was aware of a trademark claim, the designations have been capitalized.

Strong Waters includes recipes, recommendations, and tips for making a variety of alcoholic beverages. While care and caution were taken to give safe recommendations, it is impossible to predict the outcome of every recipe or recommendation. Moreover, some of the techniques presented require professional licensing and/or may not be legal in all jurisdictions. The author and the publisher disclaim all responsibility and liability in connection with the use of any of the information presented here. Readers should use personal judgment when applying the recommendations of this book.

Library of Congress Control Number: 2009938395
ISBN 978-1-61519-010-2

Cover design by Michael Fusco | michaelfuscodesign.com
Front and back cover photographs by Frankie Frankeny | FrankenyImages.com
Design by Pauline Neuwirth, Neuwirth & Associates, Inc.

Manufactured in the United States of America

Cover photo: One of the healthiest spices on the planet, ginger provides the base for a refreshing and intensely satisfying ale. (Ginger Ale, page 169)

First printing February 2010

10 9 8 7 6 5 4 3 2 1

This book is dedicated to you know who,
for all the you know whens, when we you know whatted.

Contents

Foreword

by ANYA FERNALD

MY FIRST SIP of perry was a revelation. I was standing in the backyard of a small farm in Gloucestershire, outside of a shed where bottles of perry were racked up alongside a cider press. The perry was poured into a cold glass from a smoky green bottle sealed with a plug of cork. It was fizzy, dry, sharp, and flavorful—the essence of pear filled my mouth. Before that first taste, beyond an occasional glass of hard cider, I had never thought much about the full spectrum of strong waters that this book presents.

The farm's huge pear trees dwarfed the farmhouse; the branches high overhead were speckled with tiny pears, each no longer than my thumb. These pithy, tart pears were inedible on their own, but they were central to the rich, complex flavor of the perry. I was amazed both that the possibility of creating perry had escaped me up until then, and that such a dry and unappealing fruit could become such a delicious drink after some alone time in the cellar.

The pride and excitement of the home perry producer who poured me that first glass also intrigued me—there's something about harnessing the power of fermentation for your own drinking pleasure that's thrilling. When starting a fermentation, you can control the outcome to a degree— you select the ingredients: the juice, the sugar, the yeast. Then things pass out of your hands—for example, sometimes bacteria are activated by an abundance of sugar and generate additional and highly localized flavors.

Infinite adventures can be pursued within a dark, corked bottle. With patience and experimentation, you can brew a bright idea into a glassful of something wonderful. Some historic strong waters—like my first glass of perry—require specific varieties of plants and specific methods of production that are crucial to producing the beverage. But those are the exception, not the rule. *Strong Waters* will give you a sense of the guidelines, tell you where the walls are on this very large sandbox, and encourage you to jump in and play.

A lot of words have been spent describing the many possible pairings of different wines with meals and with artisan products like cheese and charcuterie. As you begin to sample and to produce other fermented beverages like beer, cider, perry, and the occasional bottle of metheglin, you may find—as I have—that these drinks are often preferable to wine for pairing with food, as they tend to be lighter, fresher, and more flexible than most wines.

Strong Waters will be a companion on your adventures in making tipple, giving you sound advice and pointers, and just enough direction to use author Scott Mansfield's tools and building blocks to develop your own skills. A world of new flavors is waiting for you—have fun!

■

Anya Fernald founded Live Culture in 2008, and, as its current director, has assisted in the development of sustainable food businesses and nonprofit organizations. With years of experience improving sustainable food in over 30 countries, Anya is known in the United States for her more recent work introducing events such as Slow Food Nation and the Eat Real Festival, which provide consumers a direct channel to acquire and learn about good food. More about Anya and her current projects can be found at livecultureco.com.

Strong Waters

1

Why Make Your Own?

NOT LONG AGO, our forebears regularly drank a rich variety of wines, ales, and aperitifs that make today's range of choices look impoverished by comparison. While most of us today peruse a wine list to choose between grape wines—a Cabernet or a Pinot Noir, for example—previous generations might have chosen between grape *wine**, *cider*, honey-based *mead*, *metheglin* (a mead with herbs added), perry (pear cider), peachy (you can guess what that was made of), or a variety of herb-based ales. Not only could this wide range of beverages be purchased from the local tavern, but homemade versions lined the cellars of many homes.

There's a tendency to think that our culture is the most advanced in history. And while that may be true for much of the technology we enjoy, it is certainly not true for either the quantity of our leisure time or the variety and quality of the drinks we enjoy.

Why the decrease in choices? Economics plays a large role: The narrower the range of finished products, the cheaper they are to mass-produce and market. It's also often cheaper to buy a finished product than to make one of similar quality at home.

----

* Words and terms that appear in the glossary are italicized when first mentioned.

But both of these trends may be reversing, at least for alcoholic beverages. The recent rise in the number of microbreweries, the expansion of varietal wine types, and the dozens of differently flavored liquors that explode onto the market each year are all signs that we consumers want more variety in what we drink. Also, the increase in the quality of home winemaking and homebrewing supplies greatly simplifies these do-it-yourself projects and provides us with a greater ability to be creative in what we consume. These changes, coupled with the increased availability of fresh, pasteurized, and frozen fruit juices, exotic herbs, spices, and other foodstuffs, mean that we have the potential for enjoying the greatest variety and quality of alcoholic beverages ever. That's why I wrote this book and why you may want to read it.

The commercialization of modern life has always enabled us to taste the good life if we were willing and able to spend enough money. But it's often inhibited us from learning how to *make* the good life ourselves. Today, many of us do-it-yourselfers don't want to just buy a jar of pasta sauce to serve our guests—we want to make sauce from scratch. We don't want to just hire a designer to come into our homes and upgrade our kitchens—we want to go to a kitchen-design center and do it ourselves. Why? Because it's fun—and ultimately more rewarding. When we make some of our own products instead of buying only those that are mass-marketed by corporations, we expand our own tastes, define our own style, and become more connected to our environment. We become more "us."

Given the symbolic place alcohol holds in our shared culture—consumed at celebrations and often accompanying important rituals or rites of passage—making our own alcoholic beverages is a particularly rich form of self-expression. The human relationship with *fermentation* is long. Some of the earliest discovered writings are Sumerian brewing instructions, and some of the earliest known paintings show people making and drinking *beer*. The regular availability of fermented beverages was one of the principal benefits in the prehistoric switch from hunting and gathering to agriculture. As people began to create and inhabit increasingly larger cities, fermented beverages saved millions of lives by killing off bacteria and providing an alternative to contaminated water. The purpose of the earliest agricultural studies was to enhance wine and beer production and quality. The process of making alcoholic beverages led to many of the first laws, to the early specialization of labor, to guilds, and later to labor unions. Both drinking and prohibitions against it have deep roots in many of our religions.

And while today almost all of us buy our alcoholic beverages ready-made and prepackaged, making them was as common as cooking dinner throughout nearly all of our history. Countries, regions, and families each had their own cherished recipes for alcoholic beverages. Most of these recipes are lost, but some of the best—at least among those that were written down—appear updated and standardized on these pages.

WHAT YOU CAN MAKE

This book includes recipes from across history and cultures. The recipes can be divided roughly into these categories:

- **Fruit wines, vegetable wines, herbal wines, and other winelike drinks** Normally wine is thought of as fermented grape juice, and a long look down the wine aisle in neighborhood superstores confirms that grape wines dominate the market. While there are normally a few token peach, blackberry, or apple versions available, these are typically cheaply made beverages that many hosts wouldn't offer to their guests. This book includes easy recipes that will produce amazing and delicious beverages, some of which include grapes and many of which do not. Also, while grape wines have had good press in recent years for their health benefits, other types of wines have other health benefits.
- **Meads, metheglins, and melomels** Some of civilization's most sacred books—such as the Bible, Quran, and Rig-Veda—contain references to honey-based beverages. Honey was believed to be a gift from heaven, a dew collected by bees that was meant to be fermented and consumed by man. Many cultures perfected

their recipes over the centuries for these divinely inspired, luscious, and eventually rare beverages.

- **Cider and perry** The recipes for many of these light and pleasant drinks are similar to those for making wine, though these take less time to complete.
- **Beers and beerlike drinks** Beer is our most widely enjoyed fermented drink. And even though U.S. beer producers can legally add dozens of chemicals, dyes, and other additives to their brews, the majority of beers consumed in this country look and taste so similar to each other that even customers who've been loyal to the same brand for years frequently can't tell theirs from another without looking at the label. However, with widely available malt syrups, it's easy to make an excellent and distinctive beer all your own. As an added benefit, it's also astonishingly cost-effective to make your own beer. For the cost of a couple of pints in a brewpub, you can make forty pints of your own. That's right, forty.
- **Infusions** Whether it's aperitifs before a fine dinner or digestifs afterward, there are dozens of interesting and wonderful infusions that you can easily make and tailor to your tastes and to the seasons.

This book focuses on simple methods of production that require the minimum effort for maximum results for a broad range of beverages. For example, although you could collect apples, crush them into pomace, put them into a cider press, squeeze them, and ferment the liquid into hard cider, why not buy apple juice, mix it with additional juice to get the optimum balance of flavors, and ferment it? And if you make a few batches of cider from juice and want to start from apples, buy a book on cider making and have at it! My goal is to get you started and show you how rewarding the process can be. For example, by the time you've made a few batches of wine, you may find that the perfect aperitif for a Mexican dinner is your own jalapeño wine, or that curling up in front of the fireplace in February is a little cozier with a glass of elderberry *melomel*. You won't know until you try.

EASIER THAN MAKING SOUP

If you've never before considered making your own fermented beverage—let's take wine, for example—it's probably because you envision complicated scenes like these: a seasoned grower examining grapes on the vine to determine the exact moment when the fruit should be picked; squads of workers picking them; some mechanized black box that de-stems, crushes, and presses the grapes; and an expert winemaker extracting samples from a cellar of dusty barrels.

But that's because you think of wine as mass-produced. Instead, try this vision: Buy a ½-gallon bottle of pasteurized, preservative-free grape juice, unscrew the top, and pour out 1 cup to give the fermentation room to move. Then pour in ¼ teaspoon of bread yeast and cover the bottle opening with a piece of plastic food wrap secured with a rubber band. The yeast will consume the sugar in the juice and let off carbon dioxide, and the plastic will allow the gas to burp past the rubber band. (If you screwed the top back on, the bottle would eventually pop.) Set the bottle in a bucket or in your kitchen sink, in case the fermentation overflows.

In the next day or two you'll notice the fermenting grape juice (now referred to as *must*) foaming away. After a couple more days, you'll see a layer of silt forming at the bottom of the bottle. This is sometimes called *lees,* and consists mostly of dead or hibernating yeast cells. After two weeks, the yeast will have consumed most or all of the sugar, and the bubbling will calm down considerably.

At this point, put the bottle in the refrigerator, which will make the remaining yeast dormant. After another week, when the particles drop to the bottom, gently pour out a glass, being careful not to disturb the lees at the bottom. (The lees contain B vitamins but don't taste very good.)

And the flavor? Admittedly, it's not Mouton Rothschild, but hey, this is your first batch, and the point was to show you how simple winemaking can be. Making fermented beverages can be a lot less complicated than making soup. The recipes in this book utilize simple procedures that will vastly improve the taste of whatever you make.

THE BASIC STEPS

Conceptually, making a fermented beverage is like a combination of cooking and gardening. Like cooking, you first combine and often heat the ingredients. The heat not only draws out and mixes the flavors; it sanitizes the liquid, which in beverage making is the "growing medium." Then, like gardening, you add the "seeds" (yeast) to your medium, make the temperature and environment as conducive to growth as possible, and let nature take over. Here are the basic steps to making most types of fermented beverages:

1. **Preparing for fermentation** Normally this involves either chopping or juicing fruits or vegetables, boiling grains or malt, adding honey or malt extract to water, or otherwise creating a sugary solution for the yeast to feed on. This step also includes sanitizing the solution, usually by either heating it or adding a sulfur-based chemical called a *sulfite*. Sanitizing the solution helps keep wild yeast and bacteria from growing in it. You also need to sanitize any equipment you will use, such as the fermentation vessel, can opener, spoons, and funnel.

2. **Starting the *primary fermentation*** If you use heat to sanitize the solution, you need to let it cool before adding yeast; if you add a sulfite to sanitize the solution, you need to let it dissipate for twenty-four hours before adding yeast to start the fermentation. Once you add the yeast, it reproduces, making the liquid cloudy. It then consumes the sugar, which makes the liquid bubble.

3. **Racking to a *secondary fermentation* container** Just like fruit trees need pruning and flowers need old seed heads removed, beverages that ferment for longer than two weeks need to be *racked*. This means you siphon or otherwise transfer the still-fermenting liquid away from the dead yeast cells and other solids that accumulate at the bottom of the container. This cycle of fermenting and racking ends when the yeast has consumed the available sugar.

4. **Stabilizing, clearing, bottling, and aging.** After the yeast has converted the sugar into alcohol, you can stabilize the beverage by adding a sulfite. This suspends the activity of the yeast and any bacteria that might still be active. Then, as the beverage sits quietly for a few days or months, the remaining particles gradually drop to the bottom, and some harsh flavors mellow. When all or nearly all of the solids settle and the beverage is *clear*, siphon the finished beverage into bottles and seal them. The last bottle will likely be only partially full, which gives you an opportunity to sample what the beverage is like before aging. The taste of most beverages improves with aging. But there's no hard and fast rule about waiting.

GETTING STARTED

The earlier section "Easier Than Making Soup" (page 5) presented a bare-bones list of what is needed to make a batch of wine: basically a bottle of grape juice, some yeast, a piece of plastic food wrap, and a rubber band. If you followed the instructions, the resulting wine wasn't very good, but it showed you how easy the process is. Now it's time to learn how to make a *good* beverage. As you might imagine, as in other crafts, having the right ingredients and equipment and using the right techniques makes the process easier and the results better.

2

Equipment

GENERALLY SPEAKING, ALL you need to make an alcoholic beverage is a liquid containing some form of sugar, and yeast to consume the sugar and turn it into alcohol. In order to complete this process, called fermentation, you also need a few pieces of equipment.

MUST-HAVES

Fermentation Containers

Fermentation is done in clay pots, wooden barrels, glass jugs, plastic buckets, and tanks made of concrete, stone, and stainless steel. Although the convention is not recognized by yeast, many people break fermentation into two stages—primary and secondary—and each stage often uses a different container. Keep in mind, though, that you don't necessarily need to split fermentation into stages. The entire process can be successfully accomplished in a single container, especially for low-alcohol beverages that only take a week or two to ferment, such as beer or cider.

Plastic Bucket (Primary Fermenter)

The primary fermentation often takes place in a container that has a wide removable top, such as a food-grade plastic bucket with a snap-on lid. These are available from brewing and winemaking supply stores. The removable top makes it easy to add fruit or vegetable chunks, flowers, or bags of herbs. Many feature a ribbon thermometer on the side and markings that denote gallons. More importantly, a container like this is easy to sanitize—after washing the container, pour a gallon of boiling water in the bucket, snap on the lid and slosh vigorously for a few minutes. The lid also has a hole drilled in it for an *airlock* (explained on page 10).

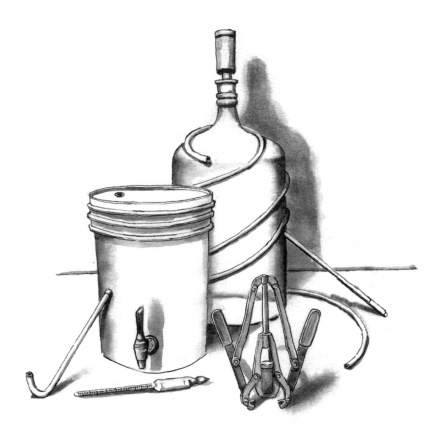

Stores or Web sites that sell homebrewing or winemaking supplies sell basic packages of the equipment you'll need.

Other Plastic Containers (Primary Fermenter)

There are many alternatives to buying a bucket from a brewing or winemaking store. You can ferment in nearly any plastic container that is made to hold food. Container stores or stores that carry kitchen supplies also offer a variety of food-grade containers—an especially good alternative if you want to make a batch that's smaller than 5 or 6 gallons. The ones appropriate for fermenting are translucent or white, with a 1 PET or PETE or a 2 HDPE recycle symbol on the bottom. The buckets you buy from homebrewing or winemaking stores are normally 2 HDPE.

One alternative is to buy a common 2.5-gallon container of distilled water, the kind with a handle on the top and a spigot on the side. Once the container is empty, cut a hole in the top, use a funnel to pour the liquid and yeast in the hole, then attach an airlock (explained below).

After the initial furious bubbling of the primary fermentation has subsided and you are ready to transfer the beverage to a secondary fermenter, simply remove your airlock and open the spigot at the bottom to drain the liquid from the primary fermenter into a secondary one. Since the spigot is normally ½ inch from the bottom of the container, most of the gunk on the bottom will stay in the container; only the clear liquid will pass into the secondary fermenter. Wash the container in hot water and reuse or recycle it.

Airlock

Also called a fermentation lock, or bubbler, an airlock is a device that enables carbon dioxide to escape a fermentation container and prevents oxygen from entering. The plastic gadget slides into a drilled-out rubber plug, which in turn fits snugly into the mouth of a *carboy* (see "Glass Carboy or Jug," page 11) or some other fermenter. Buy airlocks from a homebrewing or winemaking supply store.

You can also use a flexible plastic hose as a low-tech airlock. Fit one end of the hose into the mouth of the fermentation container and the other into a glass of water. As the carbon dioxide passes through the hose, it bubbles out of the water in the glass, preventing oxygen from coming into contact with the fermenting solution.

Plugs

Insert a plug into the hole drilled into the lid of the primary fermenter or the neck of a carboy. You'll need two kinds of rubber plugs: drilled and solid.

- **Drilled** These have a hole drilled through them so you can insert an airlock.
- **Solid** After fermentation has stopped and you no longer need an airlock, you can plug the fermenter with a solid, undrilled plug.

Glass Carboy or Jug (Secondary Fermenter)

For *secondary fermentation*, get the glass version of a watercooler bottle, called a carboy. These are available in sizes ranging from 3 to 6½ gallons. You can also use a 1-gallon glass jug, which is nice when you're starting out because you can make smaller batches. Normally you use carboys and jugs as secondary fermenters because they are glass and easily sealed, which helps prevent oxygen from getting to the beverage. Because their shape also makes them hard to clean, they aren't normally used for primary fermentation, especially for recipes using ingredients like fruit and herbs.

Siphon Hose

You need about 4 feet of ⅜-inch clear plastic hose to siphon beverages from one container to another. Most hardware stores and, of course, homebrewing and winemaking supply stores sell them.

Racking Cane

A racking cane is a J-shaped plastic tube that makes siphoning the liquid out of a fermentation container much easier. A cap on one end elevates the bottom of the tube above the gunk at the bottom of the fermenter. The siphon hose attaches to the other end of the cane.

Siphon Cane

A siphon cane is an alternative to a racking cane. This J-shaped, double-walled set of plastic tubes makes siphoning even simpler. Put the cane in the fermentation container and pump it once or twice, like a trombone, to start the siphon.

Bottle Filler

Trying to fill a bottle with only a siphon hose is frustrating. Beverage flows from the end inside the bottle you are trying to fill, so how do you pull it out and get your finger over the hole before spilling liquid all over the floor? Instead, get a plastic filling wand with a spring-loaded valve on one end. Attach the siphon hose to the other end. When you press the tip of the valve against the bottom of a bottle, liquid flows out. When you release the tip, the flow stops.

Use the device to fill a bottle to the top. When you withdraw the tube, the resulting space in the bottle allows enough room to, for example, push a cork in without air pressure forcing the cork back out.

Bottles

Unless you're desperately thirsty, after a beverage has finished fermenting you need to put it into bottles of some kind. In addition to breaking your batch into more manageable serving sizes, most beverages improve with age, and it's a good idea to separate the good stuff from the junk at the bottom of the fermentation container during the aging process. There are a few considerations when deciding what kind of bottle to use:

- How long will I store it?
- Is it carbonated or still?
- Who will be drinking it?

- ***How long will I store it?*** The longer you plan to store a beverage, the more strongly you should consider using glass bottles. For instance, a metheglin, an herbed honey wine that may take 6 months to lose its initial mouthwash flavor, should be stored in a wine bottle, while a perry, which is ready to start drinking in a couple of weeks, could be stored in a plastic soda bottle. Also, since ultraviolet light from the sun or fluorescent bulbs degrades beverages, you should use dark-colored bottles (brown or green glass) if you plan to store them for a long time. You can use yellow or clear bottles for those you plan to consume soon after bottling.

  Note: I fill one or two clear bottles when bottling a batch that will be aged. These enable me to see if particles drop to the bottom over time, which helps me to better know not only if I need to wait longer before bottling future batches, but also whether I need to be careful not to pour to the bottom of the other bottles in the batch.

- ***Is it carbonated or still?*** Carbonated beverages must be stored in containers designed to withstand pressure. The most common of these are beer bottles, plastic soda bottles, and Champagne-style bottles. Beer bottles have relatively thick glass and are handy, since each bottle contains a single serving. Soda bottles are inexpensive, light, and unbreakable and will safely withstand a lot of pressure. Champagne bottles are made of thicker glass than regular wine bottles. The indentation at the bottom, known as a push-up, or punt, helps to prevent high pressure from blowing out the bottom of the bottle. You need caps or Champagne corks and wire to seal them. The plastic Champagne corks are easy to use and require no special tools.

- *Who will be drinking it?* If you've made some cider or beer to keep around the house, you can siphon the beverage into plastic soda bottles and, after a couple week's aging, put them in the refrigerator. But if you're planning to serve the beverage on a special occasion or use it as a gift, you can bottle it, cork it, make labels, and, for wines, even add capsules—those plastic or metal-foil sleeves that cover the tops of the bottles. For a really special presentation, instead of using capsules, dip the tops of the bottles in a colored bottling wax and let it drip down the side.

Where do I get a lot of bottles? Each gallon of beverage will yield about five 750 ml wine bottles. After making a few batches, you'll notice the need for a steady supply of empties, especially if you give some of your stock away. Fortunately, there are a lot of places to get bottles:

- One of the easiest ways to accumulate bottles is to save them when you buy beer and wine from stores. Easier yet is to ask your family and friends to save them for you. However, the bottles are often of different shapes, colors, and sizes when you collect this way.
- Buy bottles from a homebrewing or winemaking supply store to get cases of identical bottles.
- Get bottles from restaurants or bars. After a Friday or Saturday night, many establishments have cases of bottles to recycle.
- Get them from recyclers.

However you get your bottles, select ones with flat bottoms; they will be the easiest to fill (unless you're making a carbonated beverage). Champagne-like bottles that have punts in the bottom are harder to fill because the filling wand tends to slip off the peak.

Corks

Always buy new corks; don't reuse them. Corks are available from winemaking supply stores. About 10 minutes before bottling, I normally steam the corks in a little water. This not only sanitizes the corks, but also softens them. Note that corked beverages develop a moldy *aroma* if the corks come into contact with chlorine. Therefore, if you use chlorinated tap water to soften corks, make sure that you simmer the water for several minutes to evaporate out the chlorine. Be sure not to boil corks, or even steam them, for much longer than 10 minutes, as they can get too soft and break apart when you use them.

Corks come in different lengths and compositions. Short corks are for short-term storage; long corks are for longer storage. Some corks are pure, and others are composites of plastic and cork. Many corks are treated with silicone, which makes them easier to insert and remove. Some corks come with caps on the end, which makes them easier to remove and replace, but their overall short length makes them less useful for aging wine. I usually get long composite corks, since they work well for most beverages.

Corker

While there are several styles of corkers, an inexpensive but still reliable type is called a plunger-style corker. This uses the principle of a lever to compress the cork and push it into the bottleneck. It's actually extremely simple to use. To get the feel for it, try putting a sample cork in an empty bottle or two the first time you use the device.

Caps

Homebrewing supply stores sell new steel caps; you can't reuse them. Also, don't reuse screw-top beer bottles or caps. Even with the home equipment available and your own massive strength, it's impossible to get the cap tight enough to hold a good seal.

Capper

If you will be bottling sparkling beverages, get one of these. The capper uses the principle of a lever to crimp the cap around the lip of a beer or Champagne bottle.

NICE-TO-HAVES

Hydrometer

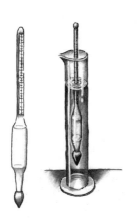

A *hydrometer* looks like a big hollow thermometer that has a graduated scale in the body of the tube and a weight in the bottom. You use it to help determine the potential percentage of alcohol in your beverage.

A hydrometer measures the density, or *specific gravity*, of a liquid. Water has a specific gravity of 1.0. The more sugar you add to it, the denser it becomes and the greater its specific gravity. Alcohol has a lower specific gravity than water, so when yeast converts the sugar in a liquid to alcohol, the specific gravity returns to about 1.0.

When you put a hydrometer in plain cool water, the ballast at the end causes it to stand upright; the water level will be close to 1.0 on the scale. If you then mix in concentrated fruit juice, malt, honey, or some other form of sugar, the liquid becomes denser, and the hydrometer floats higher in it. The graduated scale on the hydrometer indicates the higher specific gravity, and this translates into the potential alcohol level for the beverage, assuming that yeast converts all of the sugar to alcohol.

Strong Waters

In other words, if you know what the specific gravity of a liquid is before the yeast starts its sugar conversion, you can determine what the final alcohol percentage will potentially be. This also means you can, to a limited degree, increase the potential alcohol level by adding specific amounts of malt, honey, or other sugars or decrease the potential alcohol level by adding water.

Hydrometers come with instructions and are relatively inexpensive, usually between five and ten dollars. It's an especially good idea to have one when you are neither using a kit nor following a recipe, or when you want close control of a beverage's alcohol level.

I'll use a hydrometer when I'm making a recipe for the first time; if I'm making something I've made a few times before, I don't bother to use one.

Logbook

Get yourself a spiral-bound notepad, or create a computer file, and take notes. Jot down the recipes you follow, including details such as the type and amounts of ingredients, dates you did things, type of yeast used, temperatures, cooking times, specific gravity, and what the liquid tasted, looked, and smelled like at various stages. Use your powers of description. Don't just write, "12/10: Tasted like dog whiz," unless you are really familiar with that flavor. If you have concerns, such as the liquid sitting for three days without the yeast seeming to work, add that to your notes also. The more vivid and exact you make your notes, the more likely you will be able to repeat successes and avoid failures.

Also, if you do experience problems—for example, your fermentation doesn't start after a few days—the first step in troubleshooting is to compare what you did with the recipe you followed. When you rely on your memory, you'll be at a disadvantage if something goes wrong.

Straining Bag

It's easier to remove crushed fruit from a fermenting liquid if the fruit is in a bag or tied up in cheesecloth. Homebrewing supply stores sell nylon or cotton hop bags to hold hops when making beer, which are ideal for many applications. Grocery and hardware stores that sell canning supplies often stock jelly bags that can also be used. Tie herbs in muslin or two layers of cheesecloth. Be sure the bags are large enough to hold the content loosely, like a teabag, not packed tightly like a sausage.

Bottle Brushes and Washers

The biggest hassle of making fermented beverages is cleaning the bottles you put them in. Bottle brushes come in various lengths. Some of the fancier homebrewing and winemaking supply stores even sell a hose and nozzle that can be attached to a faucet.

Small Chain

About 2 or 3 feet of ⅛-inch chain is helpful for cleaning stubborn crud out of bottles and carboys. Put a few inches of water in the bottle, slip in the chain, and shake. You might want to put your hand over the bottle opening too.

Vinometer

 A vinometer is a tiny, inexpensive glass funnel used to measure the alcohol level of a noncarbonated beverage. Be aware that a vinometer is most accurate when all of the sugar in a beverage has fermented.

To use a vinometer, hold it over a sink and pour 1 teaspoon of your beverage into the top of the funnel. Wait until liquid starts to drip out of the bottom, then flip the funnel upside down. Most of the liquid will pour out of the funnel, and the rest will level off in the thermometer-like neck of the funnel. The marks on the neck of the funnel indicate the beverage's alcohol level.

You don't need to know how this gadget works to use it, but if you care, here's the explanation: Alcohol has a lower surface tension than water. So, if you stick a narrow tube in water, the liquid is pulled up the column due to the surface tension of the water and the capillary action of the tube. If you put the same tube in alcohol, the liquid will not rise as high. Therefore, the more alcohol present in your beverage, the lower the liquid will rise in a vinometer.

The problem with a vinometer is that wine has components other than water and alcohol that can affect surface tension, such as residual sugar. That's why the device works best with dry beverages: in other words, those with minimal residual sugar.

pH Test Strips

Pure water has a pH of 7.0; liquids below 7.0 are acidic; those above 7.0 are alkaline. Yeast works best (and bacteria growth is retarded) when the pH is roughly between 3.0 and 4.0 for winelike beverages and 5.0 and 6.0 for beerlike beverages. If the pH is below 3.0, fermentation may not be able to start. For beers and most fruit beverages, the pH of the fermentation solution is naturally optimal. However, for some beverages, such as mead, you will need to add acid.

Using pH test strips is an inexpensive way to measure the pH of a liquid. Some hobby stores, pharmacies, health food stores, and, of course, homebrewing stores sell them. Instructions for reading the strips are included in the package. If I'm making a recipe for the first time and the fermentation doesn't start, I might check the pH; otherwise I don't bother.

You can lower the pH (increase acidity) by adding an *acid blend*, and raise the pH (increase the alkalinity) by adding *calcium carbonate* (see page 206).

Scales

While the recipes in this book mostly use volume measures, such as teaspoons and cups, sometimes weight measures, such as ounces and pounds, are more practical. I use weight measures for ingredients such as honey, sugar, and malts. Having a kitchen scale can be handy.

Potato Masher

When fermenting stone fruits such as peaches and plums, it's a good idea to mash them. Think of it as "chewing" the food so the yeast can digest it easier.

Plastic Funnels

It's easier to add ingredients to jugs and carboys through a funnel. And plastic funnels are easier to sanitize than metal because, in a pinch, you can toss them into a bowl of water and microwave them.

Plastic Measuring Spoons and Cups

Unless you've made a particular recipe many times or it's pretty simple, you really should measure the ingredients, especially the flavorings and preservatives. Failing to measure not only increases the likelihood of making a poor batch, it also makes it more difficult to replicate an especially good one.

Degasser

As yeast ferments a liquid, it gives off carbon dioxide, which bubbles out the airlock. However, some of that gas remains suspended in the liquid. While this isn't a problem, it does leave a slight carbonation in a still beverage that you can feel on your tongue. And while there are some wine styles that use this technique to improve a drinker's experience, most drinkers find this spritz a distraction and an indication of low quality.

You can either slosh your carboy around or use a long spoon to whip the excess carbon dioxide out of a stabilized and clear beverage. There is, however, an alternative that works better than either method. Kitchen supply or beverage warehouse stores sell gadgets designed to remove the air from partially empty wine bottles to help preserve the remaining beverage. You insert the valved plug into the wine bottle, place the device on top of the plug, and pump the handle to remove the air. Remove the pump from the plug, and the remaining wine in your bottle is less likely to get oxidized. However, with a little modification, this plug and pump rig works very well to remove carbon dioxide from a freshly fermented beverage.

The valved plug is sized to fit like a cork into a wine bottle, meaning it's too small to fit snugly into the mouth of a carboy. So get yourself a drilled plug that fits your carboy and drill the hole out larger so that the valved plug fits into it.

Then put the valved plug into the drilled plug and the drilled plug into the carboy. Now start pumping the air out of your carboy. When the pump has pulled out all of the air it is capable of removing, it will start to click. At this point remove the pump from the plug and look at the carboy. In less than a minute, you'll see bubbles rising from the beverage; this is the carbon dioxide that's suspended in the liquid.

Use the pump to remove air once a day. After a few days, no more bubbles will rise from your beverage, and it will be ready to bottle.

3

Ingredients

WATER

Unless you are using a fruit that has a lot of juice, like grapes or watermelon, you'll need to add water to make a fermented beverage. The best water to use is water that tastes good to you. Avoid deionized water and distilled water, which lack the trace minerals that yeast needs to grow.

Tap water

If you like your tap water, use that. Water companies use chlorine to help keep tap water sanitary as it makes its way into our homes; although chlorine kills yeast, the amount of chlorine present in tap water is too low to prevent fermentation. Heating tap water will drive out chlorine, as will letting the water sit in an open container for a few hours.

Spring and well water

Spring water and well water often work fine. Be aware that if your water has a lot of minerals, your beverage will as well.

Note: Boiled or distilled water is flat, meaning there is no air in it. Yeast actually needs oxygen to begin fermentation. You can return air to your liquid by sloshing it around in the primary fermenter for a couple of minutes before adding the yeast.

SUGARS

Yeast is a sugar-consuming microorganism, and your choice of sugar is one of the main factors affecting the taste of the final beverage. Let's consider the dietary options for our little friends.

While the recipes in this book recommend a particular sugar, you may select other sugars to suit your tastes. The following is a partial list of sweeteners; keep your eyes open for new sources of sugar to experiment with. While exploring an Asian market, I once bought some Chinese "candy," which looked a lot like wafers of brownish sugar stacked into small bricks. I used them as the sugar base to make what turned out to be a spectacular batch of ginger ale. I've also found Mexican piloncillo an excellent sugar to use in making rhubarb wine.

Table Sugar

Chaptalization! It's against the law to do this commercially in California. In France, pfaaa, who cares? A married man or woman may chaptalize all day long, and nobody even winks.

And you, lucky person, can chaptalize like a Franco, without fear of governmental or spousal reprisal. What could be a sin in California that isn't in France? Adding sugar to grape juice increases the alcohol level or sweetness of what will become a commercial wine. Adding sugar to juices that you'll use to make homemade wine enables you to use low-sugar fruits, vegetables, and other interesting ingredients to make fermented beverages.

The process of chaptalization is named after Jean-Antoine-Claude Chaptal, an early-nineteenth-century French chemist and Minister of the Interior, who recommended sugar's use as an adjunct to strengthen, help preserve, and, of course, sweeten wine.

The chemical name for the ubiquitous white sweetener is sucrose. Table sugar is made from crushed sugar beets or sugarcane, which is then cooked in water. The resulting syrup is boiled down and refined into crystals.

Yeast, like the rest of us, has a hard time living on sucrose alone. When adding table sugar to your fermentation solution, you will need to provide it with additional acid and nitrogen. Use lemons, other citrus fruits, or powdered acid blends to increase the acid level; provide *yeast nutrient* to supply nitrogen. The recipes in this book specify these additives when the other fermenting ingredients lack them.

Since table sugar is refined, the yeast will ferment small amounts of it almost completely. The sucrose adds a slight cidery taste of its own, which makes it a good choice for lightly flavored beverages like herbed wines, but not such a good one for more strongly flavored beverages like a dark malt-based beer.

Corn Sugar

Since the 1970s, *corn sugar*, or dextrose, has found its way into many soft drinks, candies, and foodstuffs that previously used more expensive cane or beet sugar. Yeast is able to digest this sugar almost completely, even better than table sugar, and for that reason corn sugar is great for carbonating a beverage, a process also called "priming." To carbonate a beverage, after it's finished fermenting and is "still," you add a very specific, small amount of corn sugar before bottling and sealing it. Because the still-living yeast finds itself in the company of more sugar in the beverage, it digests it and gives off carbon dioxide. As the bottle is now sealed, the carbon dioxide has nowhere to go and remains suspended in the liquid, carbonating it. Again, because the yeast can digest this sugar type almost completely, there is little residue in the bottle.

Honey

Honey is one of the most amazing sugar sources on the planet. A teaspoon of honey contains nectar from between five and ten thousand flowers. If human beings had to harvest flower nectar to make honey themselves, the cost would make flawlessly cut diamonds seem like gravel. And while bees transfer the flower nectar they collect to the hive, they also do a few things that not only preserve the final product but make it a fitting fermentable base for beverages:

- They reduce the moisture of the nectar to around 20 percent.
- They add the enzyme invertase, which converts the sucrose to glucose and fructose. This is roughly the same process that barley goes through when it is malted for beer.
- They also add glucose oxidase, which increases the acidity of the honey and helps to preserve it.

Raw honey is not as consistent as the more industrialized table sugar; it varies by source and producer. It is about 75 percent fermentable sugars, so if a recipe specifies table sugar, you can multiply the quantity by 1.3 and substitute honey instead.

While the type of honey used to make beverages determines how the final product tastes, honey is the sugar source over which you exercise the least control. Let's face it: Bees wander where they will, so the workers who make your "wildflower honey" could have buzzed around any roadside weed patch that attracted their attention. There is also a marked difference between honey made in the spring and honey made in the fall, even by the same hive. To truly enjoy the honey beverages you make, accept that serendipity rules in the realm and the best honey-based beverage you ever make may be either the first batch or the hundredth. Skills and science are only two of the variables in the equation.

That said, with the rise of large farms, the consistency of honeys other than wildflower is moderately reliable. For example, clover honey is light and buckwheat is dark. Generally, you use darker honeys for stronger-flavored beverages, such as *braggot*, and milder honeys for more delicate beverages, such as metheglin.

I recommend using raw honey, which you can get at a farmer's market, instead of pasteurized honey. Raw honey contains pollen, bees' knees, wax, and other wild accoutrements. Most importantly, it has flavor. Buying honey from a farmer's market also makes it more likely that you can talk with the beekeeper. Tell him or her what you're planning to make, and the beekeeper can help you select the right honey.

Pasteurizing makes honey clearer and less likely to crystallize, but it also cooks much of the aroma out of it. After all, thousands of bees visited hundreds of thousands of flowers to give a batch of honey its particular flavor. It seems a shame to boil it away. Better to preserve it in an alcohol base and share it with your friends and family.

By the way, crystallized honey is fine for beverages. To reliquefy it, just heat it gently.

Malt

Malt is the primary sugar source for beer, though it can be used in other beverages as well. It is made from barley that was allowed to sprout. Although unsprouted grain contains some sugar, the enzymes in the moist, sprouting grain convert much of the grain's starch to sugar, making it easier for the young plant to consume. Malters, the people who make malt, monitor a batch of sprouting barley; once the growth progresses to the optimum point, the malters toast the grain, which suspends the sprouting process and adds a pleasant caramel flavor.

Malt comes in a variety of forms: crystal malt, which is the actual toasted malted grain; a syrup of malt; or dried and powdered malt. The best form for beginners to use is malt syrup, available in cans from homebrewing stores. Many varieties include hop flavoring, meaning all you need to do to make beer is simmer the syrup in the right amount of water, pour it into a primary fermenter, let it cool, and add yeast. The process is about as tough as making iced tea, and the results are more refreshing. You can spend many happy decades making beer from malt syrup, save thousands of dollars, drink the best beer you've ever had, and become a legend among your friends and family, all without using whole grains to make beer.

Raisins

In 1920, the U.S. government passed the Eighteenth Amendment, which effectively outlawed the production and sale of alcoholic beverages. Surprisingly, some California vineyards responded by increasing grape production. However, rather than make wine themselves, the vineyards shipped fresh and concentrated juice to consumers and also bricks of raisins, with the warning label that adding water and yeast could result in fermentation, and possibly wine. Thanks for the warning.

About 66 percent of the weight of raisins is fermentable sugar. This means if a recipe specifies table sugar, you can multiply the amount by 1.5 and use these mummified grapes instead. There is also an entire class of wines in which raisins are the primary source of sugar, and raisins can add character to many beverages that otherwise lack it. Be aware, though, that using any dried fruit will slow fermentation, since it will take the yeast much longer to extract the sugar from dehydrated fruit clumps than fresh juice. You can speed up the extraction process by chopping the raisins.

Brown Sugar

Brown sugar may look more natural than white sugar, but it's often nothing more than refined white sugar with molasses added. This sweetener is occasionally called for when making beers that don't include malt. It provides more flavor and more nutrients for the yeast than white sugar, but it also adds unfermentable residue to the bottom of the fermenter.

Molasses

Molasses is the residue of sugarcane or sugar beets after the crystallized portion has been drawn off. Molasses is filtered and may have sulfur added to sanitize it. Keep in mind that you may not be able to ferment any ingredient that contains sulfur.

Light molasses is roughly 90 percent sugar. Blackstrap and treacle are about 50 percent sugar and therefore leave a substantial amount of flavor and crud behind.

Molasses was a key ingredient in many old recipes, but I've found any beverage made with it is too strongly flavored. Very small amounts, however, can add interesting accents to ginger or spruce beers.

Lactose

Lactose is an unfermentable sugar that is often used to increase the sweetness of beers such as milk stouts. It can also be used to increase the sweetness of sparkling wines.

Artificial Sweeteners

There are number of sugar substitutes you can use to sweeten beverages without concern that the yeast will ferment them, such as aspartame, saccharin, and stevia. Diet plum melomel? Why not?

Fruit-flavored Syrups

Want a touch of blackberry in your Gamay? Or maybe you are looking for an easy way to enhance a mint-flavored metheglin? Since fruit-flavored syrups are pasteurized, you don't need to heat them. Sugar amounts vary from one type to another; figure between 60 to 70 percent fermentable sugar in a syrup. None of the recipes in this book include fruit syrups, so if you use them be sure to record the brand of syrup, how much you used, and the result.

YEAST

Those of us who believe in evolution understand that much of our brain is similar to that of other animals, but all life forms evolved from a shared ancestor and we have many millions of years of shared past with microorganisms like yeast. Can that have left no imprint on us? Don't think of yeast as some strange little creature you buy in a foil packet. We have a lot in common with it, including an abiding attachment to alcohol.

In 1516 Germany enacted the Reinheitsgebot, or German Purity Law. We occasionally hear about this law in beer commercials that tout adherence to this historic and noble-sounding standard. However, the law was written centuries before Pasteur proved that yeast were responsible for fermentation, and the only ingredients that constituted German beer at that time were barley, hops, and water. Brewers sometimes used brooms to stir their *worts* (malt water mixtures) and hung the brooms out to dry afterward. Unbeknownst to them, dried yeast remained on the brooms, which were used to stir and start the fermentation for subsequent batches. Fortunately, we understand the importance of yeast in making fermented beverages and can use packaged versions to make our beverages rather than whatever is stuck to the Swiffer. But what is yeast?

Yeast is a tiny fungus that eats sugar and excretes carbon dioxide, water, alcohol, and sometimes a little sulfur. Alcoholic beverages of any kind—wine, beer, whiskey, vodka, you name it—would be nonexistent without yeast. Luckily for us, yeast knows how to beat out its competitors in the rough-and-tumble world of nature. Although the breeze carries yeast and deposits it on fruit so it can feed and grow, the wind also carries yeast's competitors—bacteria, mold, and other microbes—and drops them on the same fruit. While a piece of fruit is alive and growing, these tiny organisms cling to the skin and wait. When the skin of the fruit breaks, perhaps from falling to the ground, these organisms eat the sugary interior and battle with each other for domination of their environment.

Yeast has a couple of interesting advantages here. First, when it eats sugars, it expels carbon dioxide and a little sulfur, both of which can be more than annoying to its competitors. But yeast's best weapon is the liquid it transpires: alcohol. And because alcohol effectively kills many germs, bacteria, and molds, you can see yeast packs quite a punch. By excreting carbon dioxide, sulfides, and alcohol while it feeds and reproduces, the yeast beast uses chemical warfare to subdue the competition.

Aside from our similar use of alcohol to kill germs and bacteria, we humans enjoy several of alcohol's other benefits: When used in moderation, alcohol makes us feel good, aids in digestion, and cleans fat deposits from our blood vessels. Because it evaporates readily, alcohol is also an effective way to carry aromatics to our noses and taste buds. Alcohol dissolves, preserves, and releases the subtlest and most complex aromas the natural world produces.

Some people prefer to use the natural yeasts found on fruits to make fermented beverages. Although this is risky, since the yeast may not ferment all the available sugar or could add a bad taste, it can also be rewarding. After trying a few batches and achieving some successes with store-bought yeasts, you might experiment with the natural method. The beverages that result will be local to where you made them and won't taste quite the same as a similar beverage made anywhere else.

The most famous and successful example of a naturally fermented beverage is the lambic wheat beer brewed in Belgium. For centuries, this beer has been fermented using the wild yeasts and bacteria that are native to the area. The beer is then aged, sometimes for several years. The resulting beverage is dry and has a refreshing cidery and sour flavor. There is currently a winemaking group in Northern California called the Natural Process Alliance that uses only natural yeast. In addition to avoiding commercial yeast, group members also do not use enzymes, chemical or natural additives, animal by-products, *fining* agents, or filtration.

Still, over the generations, people discovered that "cultivating" yeasts helps create consistent and tasty beverages. As with any other agri-cultural crop, we've sampled the yeast strains that occurred naturally; selected, preserved, and strengthened the ones that best served us; and found ways to suppress the others.

Like most life-forms, yeast affects and is affected by the environment it lives in. Some yeasts work better in cold weather; some tolerate moldy environments; some ferment slowly, others rapidly. Some rise to the top

Strong Waters

of a liquid as they reproduce, and others quickly sink to the bottom as fermentation slows. Some yeasts contribute a spice taste, some yield a buttery flavor, and some add a fruity or flowery *bouquet*.

Yeast is available in dried and liquid forms from homebrewing and winemaking supply stores. Both work well, though the liquid version costs more and generally starts working more quickly. I almost always use dried yeast.

When you add yeast to a fermentable liquid, it normally takes 12 to 36 hours for fermentation to begin. Before fermentation starts, you can allow the liquid to continue to have access to the air since yeast needs oxygen to replicate. In other words, rather than putting an airlock on the primary fermentation container before fermentation starts, snap the lid on the primary fermenter but leave the airlock off.

If 3 days after adding the initial yeast, you haven't seen any foam on the surface, refer to the Troubleshooting section (page 204).

Notes:

- For low-alcohol beverages like beer and cider, there are two categories of yeast: lager and ale. Lager yeast makes crisp, clean-tasting beverages, and works best when the temperature is between 45°F and 55°F. Ale yeast works in warmer environments. Most of the low-alcohol recipes in this book recommend ale yeast because it doesn't need to be refrigerated.
- Although each recipe in this book includes a suggested yeast strain, keep a few extra packets around in case the fermentation doesn't start or it finishes prematurely and you want to add a second packet. If you're making a low-alcohol beverage, such as beer or cider, get extra packets of ale yeast. If you're making anything else, get a few extra packets of Champagne yeast, since this strain will ferment liquids when others might not.

FLAVORINGS AND ADDITIVES

Herbs and Spices

Herbs and spices comprise the secrets of many closely guarded family recipes, whether the spices of a fried-chicken recipe, the various herbs it takes to make a fine gin, the type of basil used in Grandma's pesto, or the sixty-plus ingredients of aperitifs such as Campari.

In the days before synthetic medicines, herbs and spices brought not only flavor to food and drink, but vitamins, minerals, and antiviral and antibacterial properties as well. And since alcohol acts as a solvent, it can extract, retain, and preserve the essential oils in any herbs and spices in an alcoholic beverage. By the way, an herb normally comes from the leafy part of a plant, while a spice is from the seeds, fruit, roots, or bark of a plant.

In the Middle Ages, monks at the Catholic monasteries used Greek and Roman herbals, as well as their own experiments, to create mixtures called gruits, which the local brewers used for bittering agents in ales. The recipes changed based on what was ready for foraging from the forests and meadows and what seasonal tonics the local polis might need.

Some of the recipes in this book include ingredients, such as the green walnuts in nocino, that aren't typically used for cooking. These may be available in herb shops or specialty food stores. You can also gather wild ingredients yourself, which gives the resulting beverage a more local and interesting pedigree.

When using fresh herbs, remember that they will retain more flavor if fermented at a lower temperature. Another way to keep more of an herb's aroma is to let it steep in hot water for 20 to 30 minutes to make a tea, which you then add toward the end of the brewing time or primary fermentation.

Fining Agents

A fining agent is any substance added to a beverage to help *clear* it. Although the recipes in this book recommend the appropriate fining agent, as you develop your own preferences it's good to know the strengths and weaknesses of the different agents. Here are the most common types.

- **Activated charcoal** This will remove just about everything but the alcohol. If you've got a batch that is cloudy or has a musty or sulfury taste or too much *tannin*, you can use activated charcoal to strip such imperfections out. Of course, it also removes color. In the 1980s, commercial wineries used it to help make Zinfandels "white." Use 1 tablespoon per gallon.
- **Bentonite** This whitish clay is a great multipurpose fining agent, since it removes protein, yeast cells, and some tannin. *Bentonite* doesn't affect taste, though it does remove some color. It can be added at the beginning of a primary fermentation, or after the first racking if an enzyme is initially used. Soon after it's added it sinks to the bottom, but as fermentation occurs, gas bubbles lift the silty bentonite particles to the surface of the beverage. When the bubbles pop, the particles drift back to the bottom, carrying bits of fruit or other impurities to the bottom. This fining agent can remove a lot of particles during its many cycles through a ferment, so it's a good choice when you use fruit to make a beverage instead of filtered juice. You can also add it at the end of fermentation, but since there are no bubbles to circulate it, bentonite added at this stage will only remove particles once as it sinks. Mix ½ teaspoon of bentonite in ½ cup of hot water to treat 1 gallon.
- **Casein** Use this milk protein to remove bitter tannins. It won't remove as much color as *gelatin* or activated charcoal.
- **Chitosan** A seafood-based product, chitosan is made from shells and works quickly to remove proteins and tannins. Like *isinglass*, it's used after fermentation has finished, to give your beverage a final polish.
- **Egg white** This has been used by winemakers for centuries to reduce protein haze, tannins, and other bitter flavors. Because it doesn't affect color, it's especially useful with red wines. For

each gallon of beverage, use ½ teaspoon of fresh egg white gently mixed with 1 cup of the beverage and then stirred into the rest of the batch. Don't worry about getting salmonella from raw egg whites. The U.S. Department of Agriculture (USDA) estimates only about one egg in thirty thousand has salmonella, and the alcohol in the beverage would kill it if present.

- **Gelatin** This collagen-derived protein (powdered cow and pig hooves, bones, and tendons, for those of you who like plain talk) is excellent at removing tannins or other bitter flavors after a beverage has fermented. Although it adds no flavor itself, gelatin will remove some color and flavor. To treat 1 gallon of beverage, mix ¼ teaspoon of gelatin into ½ cup of cold water and heat until completely dissolved, then stir into the beverage.

- **Irish moss** Actually a kind of seaweed, use this for cooked fermentables such as beer or mead. Toss in just a pinch per gallon, 5 or 10 minutes before turning off the heat. It bonds to proteins and other particles and drags them, kicking and screaming, to the bottom of the pot.

- **Isinglass** Don't ask me how anyone thought to use powdered sturgeon guts to remove protein, yeast particles, and tannins, but let's be thankful that someone tried it. Since it removes yeast, add it after the fermentation has ended. Isinglass isn't good at clearing cloudy beverages; it's best used to give an already clear beverage a final polish.

- **Milk** Add three drops per gallon to remove tannins from white wines.

- **Polyclar (PVPP)** Though it's powdered plastic, polyvinylpolypyr-rolidone (PVPP) is quite safe and good at reducing tannins and color. Dissolve ½ teaspoon of the powder in ½ cup of hot water and stir it into your fermented beverage. It takes about a week to settle out.

- **Silica gel** This powder is excellent at clearing protein hazes without reducing color or flavor. It helps firm up the sediment at the bottom of the fermentation vessel too, which makes it easier

Strong Waters

to siphon without stirring up the lees. Stir in 1 tablespoon per gallon of fermented beverage.

- **Sparkolloid** This name-brand product is often used to clear meads and light-colored wines with very little reduction of flavor or color. For each gallon of fermented beverage, simmer 1 teaspoon of Sparkolloid in a little boiling water for 15 minutes, then stir it into the beverage.

Nutrients

Yeast benefits from having some nitrogen in its diet. Many fruit-based and most grain-based beverages contain plenty of nitrogen, but honey- or sugar-based beverages ferment better with additional nitrogen. If yeasts don't have enough nutrients, they cannot start the fermentation, or stop prematurely, or give off a rotten egg smell. You can buy yeast nutrient or booster at winemaking supply stores. Add 1 teaspoon of any of these nutrients to a gallon batch.

Other Additives

- **Acid blend** When using fruits, vegetables, or flowers that have no acid, you can add 1 to 1½ teaspoons per gallon. Light and dry beverages need less acid than heavy, sweet ones. Acid blends are a combination of tartaric, citric, and malic acids and are available from home winemaking suppliers.
- **Citric acid** Although acid blend lowers the pH, there is often no pronounced flavor. If you want to add a citrus flavor to a beverage, add *citric acid*. Citric acid is a relatively common food additive and preservative, and some markets carry it in the same section as canning supplies.
- **Enzymes** These are a type of protein that facilitates biochemical reactions. Those listed below are used when making beverages. Get them from winemaking suppliers.
  - ■ **Pectin enzymes** Many types of fruits contain *pectin*. While helpful for making jellies, pectin can cause a haze

in beverages. This haze can be greatly reduced by adding a *pectin enzyme* to the beverage before or during the primary fermentation. Use ½ teaspoon per gallon.

- **Maceration enzymes** When making a beverage out of fruits or vegetables, you normally mash the fruit to make it easier for the yeast to consume the sugar and make alcohol. In the process, the enzymes in the fruit also add color and flavor to the beverage. You can enhance both color and flavor by adding 1 teaspoon of this enzyme per gallon before or during the primary fermentation stage.

- **Malolactic fermentation prevention enzyme (lysozyme)** Use this to help prevent a beverage from passing through *malolactic fermentation*. This is used in very small amounts, less than ⅛ teaspoon per gallon.

- **Amylase enzyme** Helps convert starches into fermentable sugars. Beer brewers sometimes use ¼ teaspoon per gallon to unstick a *stuck fermentation*.

Notes about enzymes:

- Since enzymes are proteins and many fining agents remove proteins, add enzymes at least 12 hours before using a fining agent.

- Enzymes don't work as well when used with sulfites. When convenient, wait at least 12 hours between using an enzyme and a sulfite.

- Enzymes work better in a warmer environment; however, high heat renders enzymes ineffective, so don't add them to a hot liquid.

- **Tannin** This not only provides *astringency* to a beverage, it also helps protect it from bacterial contamination and color changes. Some fruits, such as grapes, blackberries, and elderberries, contain this astringent substance. But beverages made from other fruits can benefit from more tannin than is found in the

Strong Waters

fruit. Tannin can easily be added to fermentable beverages by using powdered grape tannin or toasted oak sawdust, both of which are available from home winemaking supply stores.

- **Lemon or lime juice** This is another way to add acid to a beverage. Several recipes in this book include lemon or lime juice as an ingredient.

- **Glycerin** This is used in noncarbonated beverages, such as wine, for two reasons: to add *body* and to make the beverage taste sweeter without adding sugar. Too much glycerin can make a beverage taste "metallic," though, so err on the side of too little if you use this. Don't feel bad about using glycerin; yeast produces it naturally.

- **Calcium carbonate (aka precipitated chalk)** Use this powder if you want to make a beverage less acidic.

- **Campden tablets** These tablets are comprised of either potassium metabisulfite or sodium metabisulfite. One tablet will treat 1 gallon. (If using the powdered form, 1 teaspoon equals ten tablets, so ¼ teaspoon of the powder will treat 2½ gallons.) *Campden tablets* can be used at various points during a fermentation cycle:
    - Twenty-four hours before adding yeast, to prevent wild yeast and bacteria from growing in the fermentable liquid.
    - At the end of a fermentation to stop the yeast. Adding sulfites at this stage also helps prevent oxidation, spoilage, and color change.

- **Potassium sorbate** This additive helps prevent renewed fermentation or oxidation in a stable beverage and adds a slight acidic taste. Since sorbates will not stop an active fermentation, use this only after you've added a sulfite to stabilize a beverage.

4

The Full Process

IN CHAPTER 1 we looked at the basic concepts of making fermented beverages. Now let's look at each step in the process, including some simple techniques to improve the quality of your beverage.

PLANNING THE BATCH SIZE

Make lots of small batches of between 1 and 3 gallons, rather than a few big ones. There are several reasons for this:

- **You learn faster.** Reading books, talking with people, watching videos, and taking tours can help you learn how to make a delicious beverage. But living is not a spectator sport. Nothing will help you make better beverages than experience, and with smaller batches, you will get more practice.
- **You drink better stuff sooner.** If you make a small batch of wine and, after trying it, realize that it would be much better with a little more oak, you can make the adjustment in a subsequent batch relatively soon. I know groups of people who get together in the fall to mix various grape varieties and make a different wine blend

each year. They each receive about a hundred bottles. It's great fun, but if they don't like the result, they're stuck until next year.

- **Mistakes are less expensive.** Made a gallon of birch beer that tastes like liquid toothpaste? Throw it away. Spent fifty bucks on raspberries to get 10 gallons of wine so tart you could use it to strip a floor? You won't toss it; you'll spend more money and time trying to fix it. And even if you succeed in salvaging the batch, it's doubtful you'll have a recipe you would want to follow in the future. It's great to learn from mistakes, but it's less painful to learn from small ones.

- **It's easier to make something exotic.** While you might be able to pick enough violet blossoms to make ½ gallon of violet-infused wine, getting enough for several gallons is next to impossible. Making smaller batches broadens the possibilities of using interesting ingredients.

- **It's more fun.** If you are going to become good at something, you need to enjoy the process, not just the results.

SANITIZING EQUIPMENT

Everything you use to make beverages should be sanitized: the fermenting vessels, hoses, spoons, can openers, funnels, measuring spoons, bottles, and corks. There are two main methods for doing this: hot water and chemicals.

Hot Water There are few sanitizing agents simpler than boiling water, and using it to prepare plastic and metal for fermenting is pretty easy. Most common yeast and bacteria will die after at 15–30 seconds at 170°F. However, pouring boiling water (212°F) on glass containers, bottles, hydrometers, and vinometers can cause them to shatter, so don't pour boiling water on anything made of glass.

You can also sanitize bottles and utensils by putting them in a dishwasher; many models now include a sanitize setting. If the insides of bottles are otherwise clean, which the dishwasher can't accomplish, the heat from the dishwasher will sanitize them. (See the next page for how to clean bottles.)

Chemicals Use 1 teaspoon of liquid bleach in 1 gallon of water to make an effective sanitizing solution. Be sure to mix the bleach with cold water, as chlorine is volatile and hot water will cause the gas to leave the solution. Also, you'll need to rinse the bleach solution off the sanitized object before use. Note that you should never let any liquid containing chlorine, even tap water, come into contact with corks, as chlorine will activate a smelly mold in the cork. Boil any tap water for several minutes before using it to soak corks.

There are also specialized concentrates for sanitizing equipment, such as One Step, that are mixed with water but don't require rinsing. You can purchase these from home winemaking or brewing supply providers.

Lastly, you can use a solution of water and potassium metabisulfite (Campden tablets) not only to clean equipment, but also to sanitize the beverage ingredients. Use one Campden tablet, purchased from home winemaking or brewing supply providers, per gallon of water.

CLEANING USED BOTTLES

Bottles need to be sanitized before you fill them; you'll also need to clean used ones first, removing old labels and washing them out thoroughly. Here's what I do with wine bottles I want to reuse:

1. Submerge the bottles in hot soapy water and let them soak for a couple of days.
2. Examine each for mold or other crust sticking to the inside. If some crud remains in the bottle, you can try using a bottle brush to remove it. Another method is to leave a little water in the bottle, drop in a length of thin chain, and shake vigorously. If the bottle still isn't clean, recycle it.
3. While the labels are still wet, scrape them off with a knife blade, as if you were peeling potatoes. If there's any residual glue on the glass, scrub it with a scouring pad. A few bottlers use non-water-based glues that won't come off unless you use a solvent. I recycle those bottles.

4. Put the bottles in a dishwasher or one of the sanitizing solutions mentioned on page 40.

5. If you aren't going to use the sanitized bottles right away, you can store them upside down in a cardboard box to keep dirt from dropping into them. I don't bother cleaning bottles again right before using. Most bottlers don't clean new bottles before using them. If anything, they just blow any dust out of them and fill them with the beverage.

SANITIZING INGREDIENTS

In addition to sanitizing the equipment used to ferment beverages, you'll need to sanitize the ingredients too, at least those that aren't already sanitized, such as anything bottled, canned, or otherwise pasteurized.

The primary reason for all this cleanliness is to give your yeast a place to grow where it won't have to compete with bacteria or strains of wild yeast. If your beverage does get contaminated by bacteria, you'll know it. When a beverage smells like spoiled food, it means the bacteria is beating out the yeast, and it's best to dump what you have, clean up your equipment, and be more careful next time.

Fortunately, yeast is tough and tends to beat out most competitors because of its ability to live in a solution of alcohol. Also, brewers and winemakers selected the best yeast varieties over the centuries, and the ones we have now are superstars. Still, a few types of bacteria can live in a fermenting beverage, and you need to take reasonable precautions to prevent them from growing. Even slight bacterial contamination of your beverage can ruin it.

The same two methods for sanitizing equipment also apply to ingredients: heat and chemicals.

Heat works well for those beverages that require you to boil the ingredients anyway. For example, when you make a grain-based beverage like beer, you don't need to worry about chemically sanitizing the malt; just get the water boiling and add the ingredients. To pasteurize a liquid, just as with equipment, you need to thoroughly heat it to 170°F for between 15 and 30 seconds.

Chemicals work well for those beverages where heat would damage the flavor or appearance. For example, boiling fruit juices that contain pectin can cloud the final beverage.

The chemical of choice for sanitizing beverages is potassium metabisulfite, also known as sulfite. You can buy this chemical as a powder or in a convenient tablet form as Campden tablets. A single tablet of potassium metabisulfite will sanitize 1 gallon of liquid. Although adding sulfur to a beverage sounds unappetizing, the amount you use is so small that it completely dissipates during fermentation or while aging.

To sanitize your bottles, fermenters, and the equipment you use to measure and mix ingredients, rinse them in a solution of water and sulfite. Using sulfites to sanitize ingredients and equipment has the following benefits over using boiling water:

- Sulfites won't harm your skin like boiling water will.
- Sulfites help preserve beverages and prevent them from browning.
- Sulfites, unlike boiling water, have no adverse effects on pectin.
- Sulfites can be used to stop fermentation. For example, if you want your beverage to retain some sweetness, you can add a sulfite and prevent the yeast from consuming the remaining sugar.

Using boiling water has a few benefits over using sulfites:

- You don't need to buy boiling water from a specialty store.
- Sulfites can leave a sulfury taste if you use too much.
- Boiling water is nontoxic; sulfites sanitize by poisoning bacteria and yeast.

Here are a few more thoughts on using sulfites to sanitize ingredients and equipment:

- Sulfites have been safely used in the preparation of food for centuries. Many dried fruits—apricots, for example—maintain their color and flavor better if they have been treated with sulfites.

Strong Waters

There is no research showing increased rates of disease from the consumption of sulfited foods.

- Yeast gives off some sulfur as a by-product. This, in addition to alcohol, helps to kill bacteria. So in a sense, you are using a chemical similar to one that yeast produce anyway.
- Sulfites tend to dissipate over time, so the longer a beverage ages, the lower the level of sulfites.

Which approach should you choose? The answer is to experiment and develop your own preferences.

Note: Bottled juices, canned fruit, and all heat-processed foods are pasteurized and can be fermented as is. In other words, you don't need to reheat them or sulfite them. Of course, if you add other unpasteurized ingredients to the juice, you will need to sanitize the mixture.

HYDRATING THE YEAST

Much of the yeast available is dried and in packets. To activate it, all you need to do is open the packet and pour the granules into the waiting solution. Fermentation normally begins in 12 to 36 hours. Before your yeast gets started, however, the sugary solution is vulnerable to invasion by other kinds of yeast, as well as bacteria, either of which could spoil the beverage. To reduce this possibility, some people hydrate their yeast several hours ahead of time, giving it a head start, so that by the time they add the yeast it's already kicking.

To hydrate yeast, simply pour the packet into a small glass of water a couple of hours before you plan to add it to the fermentation solution. Alternatively, you could pour the yeast into a small glass of pasteurized fruit juice a day before you plan to use it; the yeast will be not only hydrated but active when it is poured into the solution.

I usually don't bother hydrating yeast; the strains available are reliable and start quickly.

CONTROLLING THE TEMPERATURE

Yeast's growth is accelerated or slowed by temperature. Most yeast strains work best when the temperature is between 60°F and 80°F. Generally, the lighter the beverage, the more a lower temperature will help preserve aromatics. Fermenting on the warmer end of the range extracts more color and deeper flavors from the ingredients. Temperatures outside of this range run the risk of stopping the fermentation. Also, temperatures higher than 80°F are more likely to produce what are called fusel alcohols. While small amounts of fusel alcohols are sometimes sought after, especially by liquor distillers, because they add a character to the brew, they are avoided in most other beverages, since they can taste "harsh." Also, they are a secondary cause of hangovers. (Dehydration is the primary cause.) And finally, as a fermentation reaches its conclusion, the remaining yeast is more sensitive to increased alcohol levels and can stop working at higher temperatures.

CONTROLLING THE LIGHT

Yeast doesn't need light to grow. In fact, all fermented beverages are compromised by exposure to ultraviolet light: Beer gets skunky, and the color of anything with fruit either washes out or browns. Therefore, keep all your beverages away from light, both when fermenting and storing them.

FERMENTING

Yeast have been fermenting sugary liquids for millions of years, so making fermented beverages is nothing humans "invented"; rather, it's something we discovered. In other words, once you've done all the prep work for the yeast, get out of the way, let nature take over, and watch. After adding the yeast, check the liquid to make sure the fermentation starts. First the liquid will become cloudy as the yeast reproduces. Then, as the yeast starts consuming the sugars, the airlock will bubble, and you may notice the liquid begin to foam, sometimes dramatically. After the initial burst of activity, much of the sugar in the liquid is replaced by alcohol, and most of the yeast will drop to the bottom of the primary fermentation container.

If you are making a low-alcohol beverage like beer or cider, the liquid may clear and be ready to bottle in a week. If you are making a beverage with a higher alcohol level, the yeast won't have consumed all of the sugar, but the fermentation will have slowed enough that you should move the beverage from the plastic primary fermenter to the glass secondary container. This brings us to our next step.

RACKING

Racking is the oldest, simplest, and most natural way to remove impurities from a beverage. Frequently it's the only method you need to use. It's also easy. Racking is the careful transfer of a beverage from one container to another so that only the clear liquid moves. The sediment, along with a small amount of clear liquid, remains in the first container. Normally, this transfer is done by siphoning the beverage from one container to another.

How often should you rack? It's a trade-off, really. A beverage can be racked anytime a thick gunk accumulates at the bottom of the container, but each time you rack, you lose some of the clear beverage. Also, the less active the fermentation—in other words, the less carbon dioxide the yeast is giving off—the more likely that the beverage will be exposed to air and oxidize during racking. Generally, if a beverage finishes fermenting in less than 2 weeks, you don't need to rack—you can just siphon it right into bottles once fermentation is complete.

- For beer or cider, siphon directly from the primary fermenter into bottles.
- For wine or mead, rack once or twice.

    Note: When you rack from one container into another, it's important to replace the oxygen above the beverage with carbon dioxide. If the liquid isn't fermenting vigorously—for example, if most of the sugar has been converted to alcohol—you can add a couple of tablespoons of sugar to the liquid. This normally gives the yeast a blast of food it can process easily, and the resulting carbon dioxide will drive the oxygen from the secondary fermentation container.

When you are making a beverage from loose fruit, such as a grape wine, use a colander to remove it before racking. See the recipe for Red Grape Wine (page 61).

How to Rack (or Bottle) Using a Siphon

Siphoning is the most common way to move a beverage from the primary fermenter to a secondary fermenter or to a bottle. You can buy a special siphon hose that includes a pumplike apparatus to get the flow of liquid going, but it's simple enough to use a plain hose with a racking cane. Siphoning liquid from a primary fermenter into a secondary fermenter at a lower height works by gravity; the weight of the fluid in the lower part of the hose below the higher container creates suction. Beginners tend

Strong Waters

to want to suck the liquid into the hose to get the siphon started. Not only will that often get you a mouthful of partially-fermented booze and yeast sludge, it's not half as simple as this better technique of filling the racking cane and hose with water before siphoning:

1. Put the primary container you are racking from on a table and the secondary container you are racking to on the floor.
2. Fill the hose and racking cane with water and hold both ends at the same height so the water doesn't spill out.
3. Put your thumb tightly over the end of the hose that will go into the lower container.
4. Put the open end of the racking cane in the *upper* container. Your thumb on the other end will keep most of the liquid in the hose.
5. Put the thumbed end of the hose into the *lower* container, remove your thumb, and let the liquid start flowing.
6. This technique works the same whether you use just a hose or include a racking cane and bottle filler while bottling. Push the lower end of the bottle filler into a drinking glass to open the valve (which starts the siphon) and let the water flow out. When the beverage begins to flow out, lift the cane (which pauses the siphon), and then start filling bottles. (See the illustration on page 53.)

STABILIZING

If you're making a carbonated beverage, like a beer or cider, skip to the bottling section (page 52). If you're making a still beverage, you'll need to stabilize the beverage by suspending the yeast activity. The following are the most common ways to stabilize a beverage.

Patience

Though letting nature take its course is not my recommended method of stabilization, here's how to go about it. Watch the airlock. If there are no bubbles for 10 minutes, remove the lock and push a stopper into the carboy. If the stopper remains in place after a week or two, move the carboy to a warmer place and wait another week to make sure that the yeast doesn't come back to life. If the stopper is still in place, *maybe* the beverage has finished fermenting.

Be aware that once sealed in a bottle, yeast can still resurrect itself, like a serial killer in a slasher movie, and wreak havoc in the darkness of your cellar—or worse, on a shelf in your kitchen. For example, say you made a batch of wine in a cool place, and, perhaps because the alcohol level was fairly high, the yeast couldn't consume all of the sugar at the cool temperature and went dormant. Years later, you give a bottle to a friend, who leaves it in the car in a hot parking lot. It's quite possible that the yeast could come back to life in the warmth, consume the residual sugar, and push the cork out of the bottle, spraying its contents all over the inside of your friend's car. Don't ask how I know this.

Potassium Metabisulfite

The surest, easiest, and most common way to stop fermentation and clear a beverage is to neutralize the yeast with a chemical like potassium metabisulfite. Home winemaking suppliers sell this in the convenient form of Campden tablets. Add one crushed tablet per gallon at the end of fermentation. In addition to shutting the yeast down, the chemical also helps inhibit bacteria growth and prevents the beverage from oxidizing. Both of these problems can change a beverage's flavor and color.

> **Note:** The U.S. government has banned the use of sodium metabisulfite in all wines made or imported into the country because of health concerns over the sodium. However, the amount of sodium in sodium sulfite is too small to be significant. If you have access to potassium metabisulfite, use that; if all you have is the sodium version, don't worry.

Strong Waters

Potassium Sorbate

Sorbates are used to inhibit the reproduction of mold and yeast in a beverage. Add potassium sorbate after all fermentation has finished, at a rate of 1 teaspoon per gallon, dissolved in 1 cup of cool water. Note that it will not stop an active fermentation, so add it after the sulfite. It can also add a waxy aroma to some beverages.

Fortify

Like the rest of us, yeast enter a state of dormancy when the level of alcohol in their environment gets too high. And different types of yeast tolerate different levels of alcohol. For example, some strains of ale yeast go dormant when the alcohol level gets above 5 percent, while wine yeast is just getting warmed up at that percentage. Some yeasts, like Champagne, function well enough until the alcohol level gets close to 20 percent.

By increasing the alcohol level, you can overwhelm the strain of yeast you are using and induce it into dormancy. A simple way to do this is to add alcohol at any stage of fermentation to suspend the yeast activity.

Ports are made in a process similar to this. The vintner adds yeast to the grape juice as usual, and fermentation begins. When the alcohol level gets to around 6 percent, the vintner adds enough brandy to raise the final alcohol level to 20 percent, which suspends the ability of the yeast to consume any more sugar. The keeping qualities of the brandy allow the port to retain the viscosity and sweetness of the must.

This is a technique that requires some science, though. Once, while racking a nearly fermented apricot wine, I siphoned off a partial bottle, added what seemed to be enough vodka to suspend the yeast, corked the bottle, and set it aside, secure in the knowledge that I'd made a portlike beverage . . . only to come home many months later, on the first hot day of the summer, to find a delicious but troublesome aroma greeting me when I opened the door. The curse of the apricot mummy had struck, pushing the cork from the bottle and blowing its spirit across the room. Thank goodness the bottle wasn't in someone's car.

CLEARING

Completely clearing a beverage is an optional step. Most of the stuff floating around a beverage is edible, and yeast and protein are good for you. You will find, however, that most people avoid drinking your colorful but slightly muddy-looking concoctions. So, for aesthetic reasons, you should clear your beverages. Most material that clouds a beverage will eventually settle out, and if you bottle a cloudy batch, expect to see sediment on the bottom of the bottles in a few months.

Time

Time is the best way to clear a beverage, hands-down. Many excellent wines are cleared and polished not through filtering or adding anything but simply through sitting in a barrel or carboy for months or years, until all the impurities sink to the bottom.

There's a great temptation to bottle a beverage as soon as it looks like it might be clear. After all, the sooner you bottle, the sooner it will age into something you'll enjoy. Here's a test for when light-colored beverages are clear enough to bottle: If you hold the cover of this book against one side of a carboy and the title isn't magnified and easier to read through the liquid when looked at from the other side, you need to wait before bottling.

It's harder to tell when darker beverages are clear. One good indication is to take a flashlight and direct the beam through the carboy. Do the edges of the beam look fuzzy or crisp? When in doubt as to whether a beverage is ready to bottle, wait.

Again, particles will settle in either the carboy or the bottle. Better to bottle when clear.

Fining Agents

You may not want to wait months or years for your beverage to clear; not all substances quickly settle to the bottom of the carboy. Those that don't can be cleared by adding what is often known as a fining agent, which naturally absorbs or otherwise attaches to tiny pieces of protein, yeast particles, and other materials and, being heavier, drops to the bottom. There are several fining agents, and each has characteristics that make it preferable in a given situation. Some can be added to a fermenting liquid, but others, especially those that could attach themselves to yeast particles, should be added to a beverage that has finished fermenting. One of the downsides to using fining agents is that some of them can absorb up to 20 times their volume in liquid, meaning that if you put 1 teaspoon of a fining agent into a beverage, it could absorb close to 20 teaspoons of liquid. This isn't a big deal when making a 5-gallon batch, but it might make a dent in a 1-gallon batch. The recipes in this book recommend specific fining agents.

Pectin Enzyme

As mentioned earlier, many types of fruits contain pectin, which can cause a haze in beverages. This haze can be greatly reduced by adding ½ teaspoon of pectin enzyme to the beverage before or during the primary fermentation. The recipes in this book recommend pectin enzymes when they would be most effective.

Chill Proofing

You may notice sandy sediment on the bottom of bottles that you refrigerate before drinking. This harmless sediment is probably tartaric acid and is only an aesthetic problem. If you want to remove the acid before bottling a beverage, move your carboy to a cold location, about 35°F, for a couple of weeks. Rack the still-cold beverage from the sediment and bottle.

Filtering

Filtering is the fastest but most expensive option for clearing a liquid. It also frequently removes flavor and color. Given the cost involved, you might want to rent equipment from a home winemaking supply before deciding to buy your own. I've never filtered anything; patience is simpler, cheaper, and less trouble.

BLENDING

One of the more advanced and fun aspects of making your own beverages is blending different flavors. Got a batch of blah Beaujolais? Think a little "berry bouquet" would improve it? Just go to your shelf and grab a bottle of your blackberry wine and start experimenting—with small amounts in a measuring cup, of course. You can even buy store-bought flavorings to create your own blends.

There's a prejudice against blending beverages, perhaps because it's avoided commercially when making fine wines. But you needn't be overly concerned about losing the purity of your own experiments; every time you make a batch, you learn something new. Just be sure to take notes. If you have a batch that didn't work as well as you had hoped, it doesn't mean you or your friends have to suffer through gallons of the stuff. Got a lemon, make lemonade!

BOTTLING

Cleanliness and organization are key for a successful bottling run. Preparing well will ensure that once you get started, you won't have to stop to get something you forgot. Here's the normal procedure:

1. Make sure the beverage is clear and stable. If you're making a still beverage and you've added the right amount of sulfite, stability isn't a problem. However, if you're making a carbonated beverage, such as beer or sparkling wine, and you haven't added

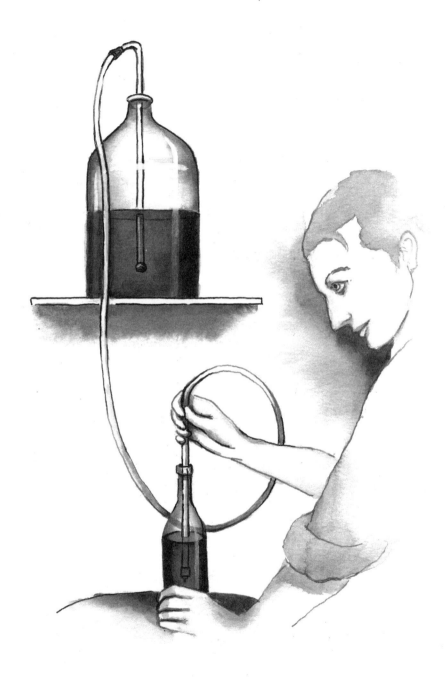

Using a racking cane, hose, and bottling wand to transfer the beverage to bottles.

a sulfite, an additional step is necessary: See "Carbonating a Beverage" (page 55).

2. Put the fermenter on an elevated spot where you will bottle. Doing this ahead of time gives any jostled particles time to settle back to the bottom.

3. If you are using caps, just toss them into boiling water and turn off the heat. If you are using corks, put a few more than you think you will need in a pot of simmering water and steam them for no more than 10 minutes to soften and sanitize them.

Note: There is a mold in natural cork that reacts with the chlorine in tap water and can cause a musty smell. Simmering the water before adding the corks will drive out the chlorine.

4. Give your bottling hose, racking cane, and bottling wand a final rinse. Make sure your corker or capper is clean and ready to go.

5. Assemble your bottles in rows on the floor below the fermenter.

6. Bring your pot of caps or steamed corks to the bottling area.

7. Get a stool to sit on; make yourself comfortable.

8. Remove the lid on the fermenter and take a good thoughtful whiff. If there's a sulfury or other bad smell, check the Trouble-shooting section (page 204) before bottling. Any problems are best addressed now.

9. If everything smells good, assemble the siphon rig and fill it with water.

10. Start your siphon and begin bottling. [See "How to Rack (or Bottle) Using a Siphon" on pages 46–47.] Fill all the bottles, then cork or cap them. Leave corked bottles upright for a week to allow the corks to set properly. You can then store the bottles on their sides.

Note: When bottling sparkling beverages, don't be in a hurry to cork or cap them immediately. The sugar you used to prime the beverage gives off carbon dioxide. Let the bottled liquid sit a few minutes, and the carbon dioxide will push the oxygen out of the bottle making it less likely that your beverage will oxidize.

Carbonating a Beverage

To make a sparkling beverage, add a precise measure of corn sugar after the beverage clears and before sealing it in bottles. The yeast in the liquid digests the sugar and gives off carbon dioxide; once the bottle is sealed, the gas remains suspended in the liquid.

When bottling a carbonated beverage, there are two approaches you can take.

You can add corn sugar directly to bottles when carbonating a beverage.

- Siphon the beverage into a separate "bottling bucket," add the corn sugar there, and then siphon it into bottles. This makes it less likely that you will siphon gunk from the bottom of the fermenter into the bottles, but it also means you have to clean the bottling bucket when you are done. There is also a risk of adding oxygen to the beverage because you're siphoning twice: once into the bottling bucket and again into the bottles.
- Bottle from the fermenter directly into the bottles, which is simpler, though some of your bottles may have a little more gunk in the bottom if you aren't careful. I would rather be a little more careful, decrease the risk of oxidizing the beverage, and spend less time siphoning and cleaning up, so here's what I do:

  Using a funnel, I add 1½ teaspoons of corn sugar to each quart bottle (or ¾ teaspoon per 12-ounce bottle) before siphoning the beverage. Alternatively, for every gallon of beverage you can mix 7 teaspoons of corn sugar into a little warm water and stir it into the beverage itself, being very careful not to disturb the yeast gunk at the bottom of the fermenter. Once mixed, siphon the beverage into the bottles.

Note: Whatever method you use, do not add sulfites to a beverage after it's finished fermenting and before you carbonate and bottle it. The sulfites will suspend the activity of the yeast, so it won't be able to carbonate the corn sugar.

AGING

Broadly speaking, beverages that have a low alcohol level or a light taste need less aging than those with a higher alcohol level or a strong taste. The recipes in this book include aging suggestions.

Note: Immediately after bottling, beverages often develop an off taste, sometimes called "bottle shock," from the sulfites that are used to stabilize the beverage. This off taste passes in a few weeks.

Strong Waters

The problem with aging a beverage is . . . you don't get to drink the stuff you just finished bottling. Gratification delayed is gratification denied. There are a couple of approaches you might take to overcome your desire to immediately consume all of a newly completed batch:

- Drink some of the batch unaged. Trust that time will improve the taste, but sacrifice some of the improvement for the joy of immediacy. Pop open a bottle after a week or two, knowing that it won't taste as good then as it will later.
- Always keep a batch of something going. After you bottle a few batches, you will always have something you made that's ready to drink or give away and be less likely to drink something before it's had a chance to properly age.

Aging in the Secondary (Bulk Aging)

Generally, there are a couple of reasons to age a beverage in the secondary container rather than bottling soon after the fermentation stops:

- Beverages that have an alcohol level above 6 percent benefit from bulk aging. And while science can explain some of what happens to a beverage while it ages in the secondary container, the time-honored and comprehensive explanation for the process of a beverage improving by aging is "magic."
- The gentlest and most natural method to clear a beverage is to let it sit quietly for several weeks or months. While you can use a fining agent to remove impurities, letting a beverage sit for a long time before bottling allows much of the particulate matter to fall to the bottom of the secondary container.

Using Oak

While the idea of wine in oak barrels is romantic, actually using them to store and age beverages at home is not. Barrels are expensive, bulky, and hard to clean. If a batch gets contaminated, you might as well use that expensive barrel to grow posies, because bacteria can hide in the wood grain indefinitely.

Rather than putting your beverage in oak, put oak in your beverage. Adding oak powder, chips, or shavings to a beverage that's fermenting or aging is a great way to add tannins and richer flavor dimensions. Oak also helps to prevent color from fading in a beverage. Using oak chips has an additional advantage over oak barrels, in that you can easily remove the chips when you taste enough oak.

By the way, if you want to add tannins as a preservative and also to give the beverage some astringency, you can buy powdered grape tannin and add it in small amounts. Both oak chips and tannin are available through home winemaking suppliers.

Note: ⬛ indicates that the recipe is pictured in the photo insert.

Strong Waters

5

Recipes

Fruit Wines

No longer drink only water, but use a little wine for the sake of your stomach and your frequent ailments.
—Timothy 1 5:23

THERE IS A difference between knowing and understanding. Someone who eats at fine restaurants may know good food when he or she tastes it, but a cook understands what makes it good. The sports fan on the sofa with a remote control may appreciate a particularly fine basketball play, but a player understands why it worked. The same is true for wines: Someone who makes good wine understands it in a way someone who only drinks it never will. If you love fine wine, try making your own. The process can be pretty simple, but more importantly, you will better appreciate what you drink. And over time, you'll learn how to make some of the best wine you'll ever taste.

Of all the beverages you can make, wine offers the biggest field to play in. From the ubiquitous but delicious grape wine to the rare tonic of elderflower wine, using fruits, vegetables, and herbs to make wine gives you the greatest opportunity to discover and develop your tastes.

Wine is the product of fermenting juice, usually fruit juice, and normally ranges from 8 to 14 percent alcohol. When selecting fresh fruit to make wine, you may have an inclination to buy the ingredients from the produce section in a grocery store. This is not usually the best choice. Stone fruits, such as peaches and nectarines, and nearly all berries are picked many days before they reach their optimum ripeness so they can better survive the trip from farm to store shelf. Generally, a fruit is as ripe as it's ever going to be the moment it's picked. Typically, the best sources of fruits for making wine are, in order of preference, homegrown, farm fresh, farmer's market, frozen, canned, and, lastly, the produce section of a grocery store. Dried fruit is often a great option, but beverages made with dried fruit are in a class of their own, as you'll see later in this chapter in the recipe for Raisin Wine (page 84).

Red Grape Wine

ABOUT EIGHT THOUSAND years ago, in the area that now includes eastern Turkey and western Iran, people began to cultivate grapes to make wine. The beverage spread all over the Middle East and led to innovations like the amphora, a container that held 6 to 8 gallons of wine and could be sealed tightly enough to prevent spoilage. This permitted wine to be aged. By Roman times the wealthy were collecting brand-name, vintage wines, and the status associated with drinking fine aged wine was established. About the same time, the divide between wine and beer drinkers was solidified: Romans drank wine, while Gauls and other savages drank beer. Wine drinking in this era was both widespread and, by today's standards, heavy. By early Christian times, Romans were consuming, on average, 1 pint a day for every man, woman, and child in the city—about 48 gallons per year. By comparison, wine consumption in the United States is currently less than 3 gallons per person per year.

Hundreds of generations of winemakers have, often unknowingly, selected the best strains of wild yeast and grapes to make wine. Modern grapes produce a juice that contains enough sugar that the resulting alcohol level ensures the beverage will keep almost indefinitely, but not so much sugar that the yeast can't consume it all. The juice also sports enough acid to keep the yeast healthy and help prevent bacterial contamination, but not so much acid, as in citrus juice, that the taste is overly tart. Finally, grape juice provides tannin, which enables wines not only to be preserved over long periods but to improve as they age. How many other foodstuffs can you think of that noticeably and naturally get better merely by collecting dust for several years on an unrefrigerated shelf?

The best wine is made from the best wine grapes. Home winemaking supply stores order shipments of grapes in season for local customers, or you can have crushed and frozen grape must or flash-pasteurized juice concentrate delivered to you year-round.

15 pounds grapes

2 Campden tablets, crushed

1 packet yeast: Pasteur Red or Lalvin 71B

1 teaspoon bentonite

1. Remove the stems from the grapes and put the fruit in the primary fermenter. Use your hands or a potato masher to crush them until all of the grapes are completely broken.

2. Stir in 1 of the crushed Campden tablets. The Campden tablet will subdue the bloom (the white film on the skins of grapes) which is actually wild yeast.

3. Snap on the fermenter lid and wait 24 hours for the Campden tablet to dissipate. Then add the packet of yeast.

4. After a day or two you should hear a gentle fizzing. At this point, attach an airlock to the fermenter to prevent the yeast from coming into contact with oxygen.

5. For the next 2 weeks, slosh the fermenter around for a couple of minutes a day or use a sanitized spoon to moisten and break up the fruit *cap* that's on top of the must. This helps the yeast come into contact with more of the fruit.

6. Seven days after fermentation begins, separate the fruit from the fermenting must.* To do this, scoop a small section of the fruit cap from the must with a sanitized colander. Hold the colander above the fermenter with one hand and, with the other hand, press the fruit in the colander to squeeze the juice back into the fermenter. Discard the pulp. Repeat this process until you've removed most of the pulp, then siphon the remaining fermenting must into a secondary fermenter.

---

* The longer the grape skins remain in contact with the fermenting must, the deeper the color and stronger the flavor of the resulting wine. This period can vary from a few days to a month.

7. Boil 1 cup of water and thoroughly mix in ½ teaspoon of bentonite. Pour this mixture into the secondary fermenter, attach the airlock, and swish the fermenter around to mix the bentonite into the wine.

8. After another week of fermenting, siphon the must from the secondary fermenter into the primary, clean the secondary, then siphon the liquid back into it. The remaining solids in the must will eventually sink.

9. When all fermentation has stopped, usually after another week or two, add the second crushed Campden tablet to stabilize the wine. At this point, the wine should clear in another 4 to 5 weeks. To expedite the process, add more fining agent right after the Campden tablet. Boil 1 cup of water and thoroughly mix in ½ teaspoon of bentonite. Then pour this mixture into the secondary fermenter, attach the airlock, and swish the fermenter around to blend the fining agent into the wine.

10. When clear, bottle and age for at least 6 months. After 3 months, try a bottle as a taste test.

Tip: Although it's a messy process, the discarded grape pulp can be mixed with honey and water to make *pyment*. See the recipe on page 138 for details.

Apple Wine

APPLES ORIGINATED AND were first cultivated in Kazakhstan, a Eurasian country between Russia and China. From there apple fans planted trees in Persia, Turkey, Palestine, Greece, Rome, and eventually everywhere they could possibly grow. Although they were universally enjoyed, apples had a reputation for causing trouble. Adam and Eve were supposedly booted from the Garden of Eden for sharing one, the Trojan War was instigated by the use of an apple, and stories of people stealing supernatural golden apples are common all over Europe and the Middle East. In spite of their dubious rep, no one faults apples' health benefits: Eating them can reduce the risk of colon, prostate, and lung cancer; they also help to lower cholesterol and prevent heart disease.

Many of the good and bad attributes of apples can also be realized by drinking them. Fermented apple juice is known as *hard cider* in the United States, but just plain *cider* in most of Europe. Since pure apple juice is relatively low in sugar, the fermented juice seldom reaches more than about 7 percent alcohol—too low to be considered a wine. So it wasn't until the widespread use of sugar that something that would be called apple wine was made.

Although you can add sugar to any apple juice to make an apple wine, making a great apple wine (or a great apple cider) requires a balance of apple varieties. One of the reasons for making small batches of wine is that it gives you the opportunity to alter your ingredients and find out what tastes best to you. This is especially true for apple wines. The recipe below makes a simple apple wine. See page 150 for more information on creating a balance of flavors.

> 1 gallon pasteurized apple juice
> 3 cups (1½ pounds) sugar
> 1 teaspoon yeast nutrient
> ½ teaspoon pectin enzyme, if using unfiltered juice

1 packet yeast: Pasteur Red, Lalvin EC-1118, or Pasteur Champagne
1 Campden tablet, crushed

1. Pour the apple juice into a sanitized primary fermenter, add the sugar, yeast nutrient, and pectin enzyme, and stir until dissolved. Since the juice has been pasteurized, there's no need to heat it or add a Campden tablet at this stage.
2. Add the yeast, snap on the fermenter lid, and attach the airlock.
3. After 2 weeks, transfer the beverage to a secondary fermenter and wait for the yeast to finish and drop to the bottom. Then stir in the crushed Campden tablet. At this point, the wine should clear in another 2 to 3 weeks.
4. Bottle and age for at least 3 months.

Note: Apples contain a lot of pectin. Unfiltered pasteurized juice is quite likely to be very cloudy. Adding pectin enzyme to unfiltered pasteurized apple juice may not completely clear the haze. Such is life.

Serving Suggestion: Served chilled in a juice glass with Stilton or a similar cheese.

FRUIT WINES

Apricot Wine

IT TOOK ME a few batches to come up with an apricot wine I like. Even when I used 100 percent apricot juice rather than an apricot "cocktail," there wasn't enough fruit flavor in the finished wine. One technique that helped me produce a beverage that reasonably astute people could identify as apricot wine was adding diced dried apricots to the primary fermenter. Be sure to use unsulfured fruits. Though they don't look as appetizing, your yeast will be able to munch on them more easily than their more brightly colored but sulfured brethren.

> 1 pound unsulfured dried apricots, diced (3 cups)
>
> 1 gallon pasteurized apricot juice
>
> 2 cups (1 pound) sugar
>
> 1 teaspoon yeast nutrient
>
> ½ teaspoon pectin enzyme, if using unfiltered juice
>
> 1 packet yeast: Pasteur Red, Lalvin EC-1118, or Pasteur
>   Champagne
>
> 1 Campden tablet, crushed
>
> ½ teaspoon bentonite

1. Put the apricots in a nylon straining bag and steam them for 10 minutes in a small amount of water. This is primarily to sanitize them, though the hot water will also help to rehydrate them.

2. Put the juice, sugar, and yeast nutrient in the primary fermenter and stir until the sugar dissolves. If the juice is cloudy, stir in the pectin enzyme.

3. Add the bag of fruit, then add the yeast, snap on the fermenter lid, and attach the airlock.

4. For the next few days, slosh the fermenter around or use a sanitized spoon to flip and moisten the bag. This helps the yeast come into contact with more of the fruit.

5. After 2 weeks, remove the bag of fruit, squeezing it gently to extract as much liquid as possible without pressing out any of the solids. Transfer the beverage to a secondary fermenter.

6. When all fermentation has stopped, usually after another 2 or 3 weeks, stir in the crushed Campden tablet. At this point, the wine should clear in another 2 to 3 weeks. To expedite the process, add a fining agent right after the Campden tablet. Boil 1 cup of water and thoroughly mix in ½ teaspoon of bentonite. Then pour this mixture into the fermenter, attach the airlock, and swish the fermenter around to mix the bentonite into the wine.

7. When clear, bottle and age for at least 3 months.

Serving Suggestion: Serve lightly chilled in a white wine glass with pork dishes or grilled fish.

Cherry Wine

FRUIT WINES

BECAUSE CHERRIES HAVE antioxidants, they are effective for fighting cancer and heart disease. They have also proven therapeutic for alleviating the pain of gout and arthritis, as well as pain due to repetitive exercise, such as running.

You'll notice that this recipe calls for 5 pounds of fruit per gallon, which works out to 1 pound of cherries per bottle. My experience using cherries has been that, like apricots, for example, they don't provide as much flavor as I think they will. The additional fruit recommended here, as well as the additional time in the primary fermenter, helps to ensure that the fruit flavor infuses the wine.

> **3 quarts water**
> **5 cups (2½ pounds) sugar**
> **1 teaspoon yeast nutrient**
> **½ teaspoon grape tannin, or a cup of black tea**
> **5 pounds black or Bing cherries, pitted and chopped (15 cups)**
> **½ teaspoon pectin enzyme**
> **1 packet yeast: Pasteur Red or Pasteur Champagne**
> **1 Campden tablet, crushed**
> **½ teaspoon bentonite**

1. Heat the water, add the sugar, yeast nutrient, and grape tannin (or tea) and stir until dissolved. Turn off the heat.

2. Put the cherries in a nylon straining bag and put the bag in the primary fermenter. Pour in the hot liquid. Mash the bag lightly with a potato masher.

3. When the liquid has cooled to room temperature, stir in the pectin enzyme, then add the yeast. Snap on the fermenter lid and attach the airlock.

4. For the next few days, slosh the fermenter around or use a sanitized spoon to flip and moisten the bag. There's a lot of fruit in this beverage, and the yeast needs access to do its job.

5. After 10 days, remove the bag of fruit from the fermenting must, squeezing it gently to extract as much liquid as possible without pressing out any of the solids. Transfer the liquid to a secondary fermenter.

6. When all fermentation has stopped, usually after another 2 or 3 weeks, stir in the crushed Campden tablet. The wine should clear in another 2 to 3 weeks. To expedite the process, add a fining agent right after the Campden tablet. Boil 1 cup of water and thoroughly mix in ½ teaspoon of bentonite. Then pour this mixture into the fermenter, attach the airlock, and swish the fermenter around to mix the bentonite into the wine.

7. When clear, bottle and age for at least 4 months.

Hints:

- Many health food stores sell tart cherry juice as a nutritional supplement or sports drink. I haven't tried it myself and can't suggest amounts, but the juice could be included as an ingredient in this recipe.
- You can also make sparkling cherry wine by mixing store-bought cherry juice with Chardonnay juice (from a kit) in a ratio of 1:2.

Serving Suggestion: Serve at room temperature in a red wine glass with chocolate desserts.

Blackberry Wine

IN MOST PARTS of the United States, blackberry brambles thrive in low areas and on the banks of rivers and streams. Most people consider them, when they think of them at all, as a nuisance, since they impede access to a view of running water.

For the winemaker though, these hedges provide ready access to delicious fruit. Compared to foraging, buying the berries is expensive, even in season. And while you can find them frozen in bulk, picking them fresh can be a rewarding effort—especially if you are into body piercing.

> 1 gallon water
> 3 cups (1½ pounds) sugar
> 4 pounds blackberries (12 cups)
> 1 12-ounce container of frozen white grape juice
>   concentrate, thawed
> ½ teaspoon pectin enzyme
> 1 packet yeast: Pasteur Red
> 1 Campden tablet, crushed

1. Heat the water to a boil, add the sugar, and stir until dissolved. Turn off the heat.
2. Put the fruit in a nylon straining bag, put the bag into the primary fermenter, and mash the bag with a potato masher until all the berries are broken.
3. Pour the hot liquid into the fermenter. Stir in the white grape juice concentrate.
4. When the liquid has cooled to room temperature, stir in the pectin enzyme, then add the yeast. Snap on the fermenter lid and attach the airlock.
5. For the next few days, slosh the fermenter around or use a sanitized spoon to flip and moisten the bag. This helps the yeast come into contact with more of the fruit.

6. After 1 week, remove the bag of fruit from the fermenting must, squeezing it gently to extract as much liquid as possible without pressing out any of the fruit. Siphon the liquid to a secondary fermenter.

7. When all fermentation has stopped, usually after another 2 or 3 weeks, add the crushed Campden tablet. At this point, the wine should clear in another 3 to 4 weeks.

8. When clear, bottle and age for at least 3 months.

Hint: This recipe also works well with loganberries or strawberries [ ].

Serving Suggestion: Serve at room temperature in a red wine glass with strong cheeses or chocolate desserts.

Fig Wine

FIGS GROW IN only a few parts of the country, but where they do grow they are frequently thought of as a nuisance, because even a small fig tree produces much more fruit than its neighbors can use. Unless, of course, you *drink* the fruit.

People have cultivated figs for at least six thousand years; the trees may have first been farmed in Egypt. Figs spread to ancient Crete and Greece, where they became a staple foodstuff in the diet of many Greeks. Figs were held in such esteem by the Greeks that they created laws forbidding the export of the best quality fruit. In ancient Rome, figs were considered sacred. According to Roman myth, the wolf that nurtured the twin founders of the city, Romulus and Remus, rested under a fig tree. Farther east, Buddha achieved enlightenment while sitting under a bo tree, a kind of fig.

Figs were later introduced to other regions of the Mediterranean by Romans and assorted other conquerors. The Spaniards brought them to the Western hemisphere in the early 1700s. Today, California, Spain, Turkey, and Greece export figs to the rest of the world.

Figs contain a lot of calcium, iron, phosphorus, and potassium, as well as vitamins C and B.

> 1 gallon water
> 1 cup (8 ounces) sugar
> 1 teaspoon yeast nutrient
> ½ teaspoon grape tannin, or a cup of black tea
> ½ teaspoon acid blend
> 4 pounds fresh figs (12 cups), or 3 pounds dried figs (9 cups)
> 1 packet yeast: Pasteur Champagne
> 1 Campden tablet, crushed
> ½ teaspoon bentonite

1. Heat the water to a boil, add the sugar, yeast nutrient, tannin (or tea), and acid blend, and stir until dissolved. Turn off the heat.

2. Wash the figs, trim off the stems and any unripe sections, and chop the remaining fruit. Put the fruit in a nylon straining bag and put the bag in the primary fermenter.

3. Pour the hot liquid into the primary fermenter.

4. When the liquid has cooled to room temperature, add the yeast, snap on the fermenter lid, and attach the airlock.

5. For the next few days, slosh the fermenter around or use a sanitized spoon to flip and moisten the bag of fruit. This helps the yeast come into contact with more of the fruit.

6. After 10 days, remove the bag from the fermenting must, squeezing it gently to extract as much liquid as possible without pressing out any of the solids. Transfer the liquid to the secondary fermenter.

7. When all fermentation has stopped, usually after another 2 or 3 weeks, add the crushed Campden tablet. The wine should clear in another 2 to 3 weeks. To expedite the process, add a fining agent right after the Campden tablet. Boil 1 cup of water and thoroughly mix in ½ teaspoon of bentonite. Then pour this mixture into the fermenter, attach the airlock, and swish the fermenter around to mix the bentonite into the wine.

8. When clear, bottle and age for at least 3 months.

Serving Suggestion: Serve at room temperature in a juice glass with Mediterranean or Middle Eastern food.

Palm Wine

PALM TREES ORIGINATED in the Middle East and Africa, and you might think that people in those climates drink palm wine because they don't have access to grape wine. You would be wrong about that. Societies that have access to grape and palm wine appreciate both.

Palm wine is made from both the fruit and the sap, and this recipe combines the ingredients. While you can't find palm sap or syrup, some health food or Indian grocery stores sell jaggery, also known as gur, a sugar traditionally made from date palm sap. Check the label, as this sugar is also sometimes produced from sugarcane. Both the fruit and the unrefined palm sugar contain vitamins and minerals. The fruit is an especially good source of iron, potassium, calcium, magnesium, copper, thiamin, riboflavin, biotin, folic acid, and ascorbic acid. The fruit also has tannin, so this strong and spicy wine will age well.

> 1 gallon water
>
> 4 cups (2 pounds) jaggery
>
> 1 teaspoon acid blend
>
> 1 teaspoon yeast nutrient
>
> 2 pounds pitted dates, chopped (6 cups)
>
> Juice of 2 limes
>
> 1 package yeast: Pasteur Champagne or Premier Cuvée
>
> 1 teaspoon bentonite
>
> 1 Campden tablet, crushed

1. Heat the water to a boil, add the jaggery chunks, and stir until the sugar is dissolved.
2. Turn off the heat and stir in the acid blend and yeast nutrient.
3. Put the dates into a nylon straining bag and place it in the primary fermenter. Pour the hot liquid into the primary fermenter.

4. When the liquid has cooled to room temperature, stir in the lime juice and add the yeast. Snap on the fermenter lid and attach the airlock.

5. For the next few days, slosh the fermenter around or use a sanitized spoon to flip and moisten the bag. This helps the yeast come into contact with more of the fruit.

6. Let the mixture ferment for 2 weeks, then remove the bag of dates, squeezing the bag gently to extract as much liquid as possible without pressing out any of the solids. Transfer the liquid to a secondary fermenter. Boil 1 cup of water and thoroughly mix in ½ teaspoon of bentonite. Then pour this mixture into the fermenter, attach the airlock, and swish the fermenter around to mix the fining agent into the wine. This wine is especially cloudy, and adding some fining agent while it's still fermenting will help clear it.

7. When all fermentation has stopped, usually after another 4 or 5 weeks, add the crushed Campden tablet. Boil 1 cup of water and thoroughly mix in another ½ teaspoon of bentonite. Then pour this mixture into the fermenter, attach the airlock, and swish the fermenter around to mix the fining agent into the wine.

8. When the beverage is moderately clear, or when you get tired of waiting, bottle and age for at least 6 months.

Serving Suggestion: Serve at room temperature in a juice glass with Middle Eastern food.

Elderberry Wine   📷

ELDERBERRY HAS AN extraordinary reputation. In ancient Sicily, branches from the tree were hung on a house to protect it from robbers. In Russia, elderberry branches protected a house from witches. The people in England, France, and Bulgaria all used elderberry for similar types of protection.

Medieval Christians, perhaps reacting to elderberry's supernatural prowess, spread the rumor that the tree was used to make the True Cross—that is, the cross that was used to crucify Jesus. The tree was also nicknamed the "Judas tree" because Judas was said to have hung himself from it.

In Denmark you could supposedly see the King of Fairyland and his entourage if you were to stand under the tree on Midsummer's Eve. The Danes believed that the tree was inhabited by a dryad, or tree nymph, named Hyldemoer (Elder Mother). It was thought prudent to ask her permission before gathering any wood or fruit.

The berries seem well worth asking for. Ancient herbalists—as well as the world's first official doctor, Hippocrates—recommended elderberry to alleviate the symptoms of colds and flu. Recent scientific findings confirm that elderberries have significant antiviral and antioxidant properties, help protect the immune system, and are anti-inflammatory.

But in addition to protecting you from robbers, witches, the flu, and arthritis, elderberry has another great attribute: You can make superb wine from both the blossoms and the berries.

While you can't find this fruit in stores or even at farmers' markets, you can easily pick gallons of elderberries in mid- to late summer from the shrublike trees that are found in fields, by streams, and at the forest's edge. Since the flavor can vary quite a bit from one stand of bushes to the next, it's not a bad idea to sample berries from different areas before committing to a few hours' worth of picking.

The fresh or dried berries can be made into a gorgeous dark wine with a flavor reminiscent of black cherries and resembling a Chianti or port.

In fact, elderberries were so commonly used to help improve the quality of fake port that their cultivation was outlawed in Portugal in the late eighteenth century.

And partly because the berries contain a substantial amount of tannin, the wine can be aged for many years.

1 pound bananas, sliced (3 cups)

1 gallon water

6 cups (3 pounds) sugar

1 teaspoon yeast nutrient

3 pounds fresh elderberries (9 cups)

½ teaspoon pectin enzyme

1 packet yeast: Pasteur Red, Lalvin 71B, or Lalvin RC212

½ teaspoon gelatin

1 Campden tablet, crushed

½ teaspoon bentonite

1. Simmer the banana slices in the water for 30 minutes. Strain the liquid, discarding the solids, and stir in the sugar and yeast nutrient.
2. Carefully strip the berries from their stems. Rinse the berries and sort through them to remove any that are unripe.
3. Pour the berries into a nylon straining bag, put the bag in the primary fermenter, and mash the berries, being careful not to crack the seeds.
4. Pour the hot liquid over the fruit.
5. When the liquid has cooled to room temperature, stir in the pectin enzyme, then add the yeast. Snap on the fermenter lid and attach the airlock.
6. For the next few days, slosh the fermenter around or use a sanitized spoon to flip and moisten the bag of fruit. This helps the yeast come into contact with more of the fruit.

7. One week after fermentation starts, remove the bag of berries from the fermenting must, squeezing it gently to extract as much liquid as possible without pressing out any of the solids. Transfer the liquid to a secondary fermenter. Dissolve the gelatin in ½ cup of hot water and add it to fermenter. (This wine has a lot of color and sufficient tannin, so adding a fining agent now will help it clear better.)

8. When all fermentation has stopped, usually after another 2 or 3 weeks, add the crushed Campden tablet. At this point, the wine should clear in another 2 to 3 weeks. To expedite the process, add a fining agent right after the Campden tablet. Boil 1 cup of water and thoroughly mix in ½ teaspoon of bentonite. Then pour this mixture into the fermenter, attach the airlock, and swish the fermenter around to mix the fining agent into the wine.

9. When clear, bottle and age for at least 3 months.

Tips:

- The berries are easier to remove from the stems when slightly frozen.
- You can use fewer fresh elderberries, 2 pounds per gallon minimum, for a lighter wine.
- You can substitute 1 pound (2½ cups) of dried elderberries for the fresh. Put them in a nylon bag and pour the hot liquid on them in the primary fermenter. Don't mash them. Leave them for a total of 10 days before removing them and transferring the liquid to the secondary fermenter. You can buy the dried berries from herb shops.

Serving Suggestion: Elderberry wine is a great alternative for afternoon tea, served with scones, finger sandwiches, muffins, or coffee cake. It also makes an excellent accompaniment to dessert. Serve at room temperature in a port glass.

Pomegranate Wine

I would lead thee, and bring thee into my mother's house, who would instruct me: I would cause thee to drink of spiced wine of the juice of my pomegranate.
—*Song of Solomon 8:2*

WHILE WE MIGHT suspect that there is a bit more to this woman's invitation than having her man over for a tipple, this biblical passage does show that pomegranate was once commonly used to make wine.

Greek mythology also refers to the pomegranate as a means to inspire romantic attachment. Hades, the lord of the underworld, kidnapped the lovely Persephone. When her mother, Demeter, found out about the abduction, she pleaded with Zeus to let her daughter return. Zeus agreed that she could, providing she had not tasted any of the fruit of the underworld. Since Persephone had nibbled a bit of pomegranate that Hades had given her, she was forever bound to him.

Until relatively recently, about the only way many drinkers consumed pomegranates was in cocktails, such as the tequila sunrise, that include the sugary pomegranate syrup called grenadine. In the early twenty-first century, however, nutritionists and pomegranate growers touted the fruit juice as an elixir that improves heart health, lowers hypertension, eases the difficulties of menopause, and fights breast and prostate cancer.

The actual fruit, if you haven't seen the inside of one, has a tough, inedible skin and lots of bitter-tasting pith separating several chambers of seeds. In fact, the fruity part of a pomegranate is the juicy membrane that covers each seed. It's a lot of mess and trouble to eat, which is one reason why your mother probably never put pomegranates in your lunch box. Although it can take a good deal of time to break the seeds free of the skin and pith, there is a bit of good news: The yeast will actually take care of the juicing for you. In other words, you don't have to crush the kernels to get at the juice.

7 pounds fresh pomegranates
2 cups (1 pound) pearled barley
1 gallon water
4 cups (2 pounds) sugar
½ teaspoon grape tannin, or a cup of black tea
1 teaspoon yeast nutrient
½ teaspoon pectin enzyme
1 packet yeast: Pasteur Champagne
1 Campden tablet, crushed

1. Cut the fruit into sections. Separate the kernels from the pith and skin, and drop them into the primary fermenter.
2. Boil the barley in 1 quart of the water for 20 minutes. Strain the hot liquid and discard the barley or save it for another use. Add the sugar, tannin (or tea), and yeast nutrient, and stir until dissolved.
3. Pour the hot liquid into the primary fermenter and add the remaining 3 quarts of water.
4. When the liquid has cooled to room temperature, stir in the pectin enzyme and add the yeast. Snap on the fermenter lid and attach the airlock.
5. For the next few days, slosh the fermenter around or use a sanitized spoon to moisten and break up the fruit cap that's on top of the must. This helps the yeast come into contact with more of the fruit.
6. After 7 days, remove the fruit from the fermenting must, using a sanitized colander to scoop out the solids. Any remaining solids will eventually sink to the bottom.

7. After another 5 days, transfer the liquid to the secondary fermenter.

8. When all fermentation has stopped, usually after another week or two, add the crushed Campden tablet. The wine should clear in another 2 to 3 weeks.

9. When clear, bottle and age for at least 3 months.

Hints:

- Separating the kernels from the rind and pith can be messy, so wear an old shirt. The easiest way to free the kernels is to use your hands. Hold sections of the fruit inside a deep bucket and use your thumbs and fingers to scrape the fruit from the rind. Pick out the larger pieces of pith that fall into the bucket, then pour enough water on the fruit to cover it. Since the pith floats and the fruit doesn't, the pith will float to the top of the water, where you can skim it out.

- It's simpler to use store-bought pomegranate juice to make this wine. A good wine can be made from half pomegranate juice and half white grape juice. I've also made stellar batches of sparkling wine with two-thirds Chardonnay juice (from a kit) and one-third pomegranate juice. Note, though, that without sulfites to protect it, the sparkling wine may turn brown after about 6 months. The taste will be fine, but the wine's color is part of the appeal.

Serving Suggestion: Serve lightly chilled in a white wine glass with soft cheeses or pasta with cream sauce.

Raspberry Wine

DELICATE, REFRESHING, ATTRACTIVE, and expensive: raspberry wine is an extravagant indulgence but one worth making to enjoy on special occasions. The berries can also be added to other wines for flavor and color.

In addition to making a gorgeous and tasty wine, raspberries have a lot of vitamin C and antibacterial properties.

> **1 pound bananas, sliced (3 cups)**
> **1 gallon water**
> **4 cups (2 pounds) sugar**
> **1 teaspoon yeast nutrient**
> **½ teaspoon grape tannin, or a cup of black tea**
> **4 pounds fresh or frozen raspberries (12 cups)**
> **½ teaspoon pectin enzyme**
> **1 packet yeast: Pasteur Red, Lalvin 71B, or Côte des Blancs**
> **1 Campden tablet, crushed**

1. Simmer the banana slices in the water for 30 minutes. Strain the liquid, discarding the solids, and stir in the sugar, yeast nutrient, and tannin (or tea).

2. Pour the raspberries into a nylon straining bag, put the bag in the primary fermenter, and mash with a potato masher until all of the berries are broken.

3. Pour in the hot liquid.

4. When the liquid cools to room temperature, stir in the pectin enzyme and add the yeast. Snap on the fermenter lid and attach the airlock.

5. For the next few days, slosh the fermenter around or use a sanitized spoon to flip and moisten the bag. This helps the yeast come into contact with more of the fruit.

6. After 1 week, remove the bag from the fermenting must, squeezing it gently to extract as much liquid as possible without pressing out any of the solids. Siphon the liquid into a secondary fermenter.

7. When all fermentation has stopped, usually after another week or two, add the crushed Campden tablet. At this point, the wine should clear in another 2 to 3 weeks.

8. When clear, bottle and age for at least 3 months.

Serving Suggestion: Serve lightly chilled in white wine glasses with creamy cheeses or between courses as a palate cleanser. This wine is also wonderful with chocolate desserts.

Raisin Wine

WHEN THE PRIMARY flavor is an exotic or expensive fruit or herb, many wine recipes include raisins as a well-balanced, convenient, and inexpensive source of sugar, acid, yeast nutrient, and tannin. But there are other recipes where dried fruit is the primary ingredient. *Stepponi*, *nectour*, *passum*, and *persenica* are all styles of raisin wine. They also have sexy Latin names. Unfortunately it seems as though the only population regularly using raisins to make wine in the United States is that of inmates in penitentiaries who refer to the libation as Pruno, regardless of the type of dried fruit used.

> 1 gallon water
>
> 1 cup (8 ounces) sugar
>
> 3 pounds raisins, chopped (8 cups)
>
> Juice and zest of 4 lemons
>
> ½ teaspoon pectin enzyme
>
> 1 packet yeast: Pasteur Champagne
>
> 1 Campden tablet, crushed
>
> ½ teaspoon bentonite

1. Heat the water to a boil, add the sugar, and stir until dissolved. Turn off the heat.
2. Put the raisins in a nylon straining bag.
3. Put the bag of fruit in the primary fermenter and pour the hot liquid over it.
4. When the liquid has cooled to room temperature, stir in the lemon juice and zest and the pectin enzyme, then add the yeast. Snap on the fermenter lid and attach the airlock.
5. For the next few days, slosh the fermenter around or use a sanitized spoon to flip and moisten the bag. This helps the yeast come into contact with more of the fruit.

6. After 2 weeks, remove the bag of fruit from the fermenting must, squeezing it gently to extract as much liquid as possible without pressing out any of the solids. Transfer the liquid to the secondary fermenter.

7. When all fermentation has stopped, usually after another 2 or 3 weeks, add the crushed Campden tablet. The wine should clear in another 3 to 4 weeks. To expedite the process, add a fining agent right after the Campden tablet. Boil 1 cup of water and thoroughly mix in ½ teaspoon of bentonite. Then pour this mixture into the fermenter, attach the airlock, and swish the fermenter around to mix the fining agent into the wine.

8. When clear, bottle and age for at least 3 months.

Hint: You can make a similar recipe using prunes, aka dried plums.

Serving Suggestion: Serve at room temperature in a port glass.

Wine Kits

People have been making wine from juice concentrates since before the Roman Empire. A syrup known as *cute* was made from juice that was reduced to two-thirds by boiling; it seems to have been commonly used in Europe to make wine until at least the seventeenth century. While the juice concentrates were cheaper to transport than wine, the quality of the wine they made was likely pretty poor.

Fortunately for us, the quality of kits has improved dramatically, and it is now possible to make truly superb wines at home with very little equipment. All of the ingredients—not merely the concentrate and the yeast, but preservatives, fining agents, counter fining agents (to remove the fining agents), and even oak chips and herbs for color and flavoring—are included in numbered, pre-measured packets. The concentrates come from the finest grape-growing regions in the world. But probably the most surprising aspect of the kits available today is their relatively low cost. Whatever quality of wine you want to make, if you make it yourself from a kit, expect to pay less than one-fifth the price compared to buying a bottled wine of similar quality from a discount beverage store. Wine kits are the best way to learn about making wines: The quality is great, the price is right, everything is included in the kit, and the instructions are simple.

Kits vary in size and quality, from 1-quart cans of concentrate to 4-gallon kits of concentrates mixed with fresh juice to pails of frozen juice and skins. I prefer the premium or super premium kits that include around 4 gallons of concentrate and make 6 gallons of wine. The juice in these kits has been analyzed in a lab and the nutrients and pH adjusted as necessary. These wines age well, just like wine made from fresh fruit.

However, I also use the less expensive kits, the ones with only 2 gallons of concentrate, since the beverages they make are ready to drink sooner. They don't age as well, but the quality is fine for making everyday wines to have with meals.

The even less expensive canned concentrates are good as a base for something more interesting, though the resulting wine isn't as good as wine from the other kits. You may want to use these in a blend; for instance, mix a blueberry wine with a base of canned grape concentrate.

Notes:
- Choosing among various kits, especially if you shop the Internet, can be daunting. A good approach is to determine the variety of wine you want to make, then use an Internet search engine to look for a "gold medal kit" of that variety. Read the descriptions, pick

your manufacturer, then search on that manufacturer and wine kit name to find the best price. Note that some wine kit providers offer free shipping, so take that into account when comparing prices.

- The amount of water you add when making a kit differs from the amount added in the recipes in this book. Follow the directions in a kit; the instructions will tell you to add water to the concentrate until the total volume of concentrate and water equals, for example, 6 gallons. You do not, to continue with the example, add 6 gallons of water to a kit that has 4 gallons of concentrate. Most good wine kits are designed to make 6 gallons; none of them make 10.

  On the other hand, most of the recipes in this book that include water instruct you to add 1 gallon. After you add the remaining ingredients, such as fruit and sugar, you will produce more than 1 gallon of wine. Standardizing the recipes to 1 gallon of added water makes measuring easier and calculations simpler when you are making larger batches.

Vegetable Wines

I KNOW WHAT you're thinking: *Finally—something to do with all of those baseball bat–sized zucchinis crawling out of the garden!* While we mostly think of vegetables of as a novelty ingredient in wine, some actually make a decent beverage. If you like the results from a couple of these recipes, branch out to using other vegetables. Carrots, beets, and peas are all supposed to make fine wines.

Sweet Potato Wine

SWEET POTATOES ARE on nearly everyone's list of the world's greatest foods, being loaded with beta-carotene, complex carbohydrates, vitamin C, B vitamins, fiber, protein, iron, and calcium. It's one of those vegetables we always make a note to eat more of but seldom do.

Every culture that has sweet potatoes has, at one time or other, used them to make wine. In the United States, the following slightly updated recipe was popular in the South after the Civil War. The pale orange wine it makes is light, with a mild citrus flavor. You don't need to go out of your way to make it; next time you cook a bunch of sweet potatoes, save the water to make this wine—one more incentive for cooking and eating a superfood.

> 1 gallon water
> 3 cups (1½ pounds) sugar
> 6 pounds sweet potatoes
> 1 pound raisins, chopped (3 cups)
> ½ teaspoon acid blend
> Juice of 1 lime
> 1 teaspoon yeast nutrient
> ½ teaspoon pectin enzyme
> ½ teaspoon grape tannin, or a cup of black tea
> 1 packet yeast: Pasteur Champagne
> 1 Campden tablet
> ½ teaspoon bentonite

1. Heat the water to a boil, add the sugar, and stir until dissolved. Stir in the potatoes, raisins, and acid blend. Lower the heat and simmer for 30 minutes.
2. Strain the liquid, using a colander, into the primary fermenter. Eat the potatoes!

3. Let the liquid cool to room temperature, then stir in the lime juice, yeast nutrient, pectin enzyme, and tannin (or tea). Add the yeast. Snap on the fermenter lid and attach the airlock.

4. After 2 weeks, transfer the liquid to a secondary fermenter.

5. When all fermentation has stopped, usually after another week or two, add the crushed Campden tablet. The wine should clear as much as it ever will in another 2 to 3 weeks. To expedite the process, add a fining agent right after the Campden tablet. Boil 1 cup of water and thoroughly mix in ½ teaspoon of bentonite. Then pour this mixture into the fermenter, attach the airlock, and swish the fermenter around to mix the fining agent into the wine.

6. Because of the protein in the sweet potatoes, don't bother waiting for this wine to totally clear. Give the bentonite a couple of weeks to drift to the bottom, then bottle it and age for at least 3 months.

Notes:

- Sweet potato, yam—what's the difference? Who cares? They both make a fine wine, and some stores mix the terms. Fortunately, these tubers are next to each other in the produce section, so when shopping, ignore the name and buy the darkest variety available. It will not only have more vitamins than its neighbors, but also make a darker colored wine.

- Because of the protein in this vegetable, the wine won't totally clear.

Serving Suggestion: Serve lightly chilled in a white wine glass with poultry or cream sauces.

Red Tomato Wine

AN OVERABUNDANCE OF TOMATOES from the late summer garden inspires desperate growers to come up with new ways to consume them. I grew up in the Midwest, and the parents or grandparents of a few of my Polish friends made a version of this wine every summer. This recipe makes a dry, rich white wine, and yes, it tastes a little like tomatoes.

> 1 **gallon water**
> 4 **cups (2 pounds) sugar**
> 1 **teaspoon yeast nutrient**
> ½ **teaspoon grape tannin, or a cup of black tea**
> 4 **pounds ripe tomatoes, sliced (about 12 cups)**
> 1 **package yeast: Pasteur Red**
> 1 **Campden tablet, crushed**

1. Heat the water to a boil, add the sugar, yeast nutrient, and tannin (or tea), and stir until dissolved. Turn off the heat.
2. Cut the tomatoes into ½-inch slices. Put them in a nylon straining bag and place it in the primary fermenter.
3. Pour the boiling liquid over the tomatoes and mash them with a potato masher.
4. When the liquid has cooled to room temperature, add the yeast. Snap on the fermenter lid and attach the airlock.
5. For the next few days, slosh the fermenter around or use a sanitized spoon to flip and moisten the bag. This helps the yeast come into contact with more of the tomatoes.
6. After 1 week, remove the bag from the fermenting must, squeezing it gently to extract as much liquid as possible without pressing out any of the solids. Transfer the liquid to a secondary fermenter.

7. When all fermentation has stopped, usually after another week or two, add the crushed Campden tablet.
8. Bottle at 3 weeks, or as soon as it's clear. Age for at least 2 months.

Serving Suggestion: Serve in an ice-cold pint glass with kielbasa at Oktoberfest. Save some of the batch for Dyngus Day, if possible. (That's the Polish–American Easter Monday, for those who haven't celebrated it before.)

Green Tomato Wine

GREEKS CALLED THE tomato *lycopersicon*, "wolf peach," and making this white wine with unripe tomatoes may be a way to give them additional teeth. Gardens that experience an early hard frost can be left with a lot of green tomatoes on a wilting vine. Green tomatoes make an interesting side dish, but can there be nothing except the fryer in their future? A less fatty disposition is to make a wine like this.

2 cups (1 pound) pearled barley

1 gallon water

6 cups (3 pounds) sugar

½ teaspoon grape tannin, or a cup of black tea

1 teaspoon yeast nutrient

4 pounds green tomatoes, sliced (about 12 cups)

1 pound raisins, chopped (3 cups)

½ teaspoon pectin enzyme

1 packet yeast: Pasteur Red

1 Campden tablet, crushed

½ teaspoon bentonite

1. Boil the barley in 1 quart of the water for 20 minutes. Strain the hot liquid and discard the barley or save it for another use. Put the barley water in a large pot, add the sugar, tannin (or tea), and yeast nutrient, and stir until dissolved.

2. Put the tomatoes and raisins into a nylon straining bag and add to the liquid. Simmer gently until the tomatoes are soft.

3. Pour the liquid into the primary fermenter along with the nylon straining bag, and mash the contents of the bag lightly with a potato masher. Add the remaining 3 quarts of water.

4. When the liquid has cooled to room temperature, stir in the pectin enzyme. Cover the fermenter with the lid.

5. Wait 24 hours, then add the yeast. Snap on the fermenter lid and attach the airlock.
6. For the next few days, slosh the fermenter around or use a sanitized spoon to flip and moisten the bag. This helps the yeast come into contact with more of the tomatoes.
7. After 10 days, remove the bag from the fermenting must, squeezing it gently to extract as much liquid as possible without pressing out any of the solids. Transfer the liquid to a secondary fermenter.
8. When all fermentation has stopped, usually after another week or two, add the crushed Campden tablet. At this point, the wine should clear in another 4 to 6 weeks. To expedite the process, add a fining agent right after the Campden tablet. Boil 1 cup of water and thoroughly mix in ½ teaspoon of bentonite. Then pour this mixture into the fermenter, attach the airlock, and swish the fermenter around to mix the fining agent into the wine.
9. When clear, bottle and age 4 to 6 months.

Serving Suggestion: Serve chilled in a juice glass with egg-based brunches or smoked meat and fish.

Jalapeño Wine

JALAPEÑOS AND OTHER hot peppers are some of the most medicinal foods available. They contain bioflavonoids and carotenoids that fight cancer. The hot ingredient in the pepper, capsaicin, has been shown to protect DNA and cells from attack by toxic substances. In addition, capsaicin helps prevent or heal the following conditions: allergies, arthritis, asthma, bleeding, colds and flus, constipation, diabetes, heart disease, hemorrhoids, high blood pressure, high cholesterol, obesity, osteoarthritis, poor circulation, and stroke. So how do you get more jalapeños in your system?

> 1 gallon water
> 4 cups (2 pounds) sugar
> 1 teaspoon yeast nutrient
> ½ teaspoon grape tannin, or a cup of black tea
> 8 ounces jalapeño peppers, sliced (1½ cups)
> 1 pound raisins (3 cups)
> 1 package yeast: Pasteur Red
> 1 Campden tablet, crushed

1. Heat the water to a boil; add the sugar, yeast nutrient, and tannin, and stir until dissolved. Turn off the heat.
2. Chop the peppers and raisins, put them in a nylon straining bag, and place it in the primary fermenter.
3. Pour the hot liquid over the bag.
4. When the liquid has cooled to room temperature, add the yeast. Snap on the fermenter lid and attach the airlock.
5. After 2 days, remove the bag, squeezing it gently to extract as much liquid as possible without pressing out any of the solids. Transfer the liquid to a secondary fermenter.

6. When all fermentation has stopped, usually after another week or two, add the crushed Campden tablet. The wine should clear in another 2 to 3 weeks.
7. Bottle and age for at least 2 months.

Serving Suggestion: Serve lightly chilled in a digestif glass after a Mexican meal. This wine also makes a stupendous marinade for meat.

Rhubarb Wine

YOU CAN MAKE a gorgeous and healthful wine from rhubarb stalks. Note that this wine may not clear completely, but don't let that stop you from making it. This recipe creates a tart, dry, and altogether refreshing wine.

Rhubarb in one form or another has been used as a medicinal plant as far back as the third millennium BC in China and as recently as the last century. One of its most celebrated cures was for a seventeenth-century Guangzong emperor who apparently suffered a severe illness after having sex with four beautiful women.

Arabs and Europeans also recognized the therapeutic effects of the Chinese species, aside from its postcoital cathartic qualities, and eagerly bought as much of it as Asia would part with. By the nineteenth century, the Chinese were using Europe's rhubarb dependency for political and trade leverage. In 1839, Lin Zexu, the Imperial commissioner, tried to put an end to British opium trafficking in China. He wrote a letter to Queen Victoria threatening to withhold shipments of rhubarb and tea, the effect of which would surely lead to the deaths of many foreign barbarians, if British merchants did not stop trading in opium. Victoria didn't respond. When Lin Zexu sent a similar letter to the British merchants, they responded with gunboats.

Fortunately we no longer need to fight over access to rhubarb; a hybrid variety grows in many countries outside of China.

4 pounds rhubarb stalks, diced (about 14 cups)

6 cups (3 pounds) sugar

1 gallon boiling water

1 teaspoon yeast nutrient

¼ teaspoon grape tannin, or a cup of black tea

1 packet yeast: Pasteur Champagne or Pasteur Red

½ teaspoon pectin enzyme

1 Campden tablet, crushed
½ teaspoon bentonite

1. Put the rhubarb in a nylon straining bag. Before tying the bag shut, set it in the primary fermenter and pour in enough of the sugar to cover the rhubarb. Tie the bag shut and pour the remaining sugar over the bag, letting it sift through the cloth and onto the rhubarb. Leave the fruit and sugar in the fermenter for 6 to 10 hours. The sugar will soften the fruit.

2. Pour the boiling water over the fruit and sugar. Stir well and make sure that all the sugar is dissolved. Stir in the yeast nutrient and tannin (or tea). After 20 minutes, mash the rhubarb with a potato masher.

3. When the liquid has cooled to room temperature, stir in the pectin enzyme, then add the yeast. Snap on the fermenter lid and attach the airlock.

4. For the next few days, slosh the fermenter around or use a sanitized spoon to flip and moisten the bag. This helps the yeast come into contact with more of the rhubarb.

5. After 2 weeks, remove the bag, squeezing it gently to extract as much liquid as possible without pressing out any of the solids. Transfer the liquid to a secondary fermenter.

6. When all fermentation has stopped, usually after another week or two, add the crushed Campden tablet. Swish the fermenter around to mix it in.

7. When clear, bottle and age for at least 6 months.

Note: I've made this wine several times using different methods, and it's always hazy. You can use bentonite to clear it somewhat, but be aware that this and most fining agents will remove some color and tannin. This wine's color is pretty light anyway, so you may want to just wait it out. If you do want to try clearing it, in step 5, boil 1 cup of water and thoroughly mix in ½ teaspoon of bentonite. Then pour this mixture into the secondary fermenter, attach the airlock, and swish the fermenter around to mix the fining agent into the wine.

Serving Suggestion: Serve lightly chilled in white wine glass with cheese appetizers, poultry, or pork.

Miscellaneous Wines

MAKING WINE WITH flavorings such as herbs, flowers, and leaves is more challenging than making it from fruit or vegetables, not only because many of these plants have few fermentable sugars of their own, but also because their flavors tend to be more delicate and easily lost during fermentation.

Although this chapter covers miscellaneous wines, its particular focus is on flower and herb wines, which have been highly valued as digestives and tonics by generations of knowledgeable and happy consumers. They are also among the most exotic beverages most people will ever consume.

Making flower wines presents exceptional challenges. Flowers have a particularly short season; a field of blossoms may bloom for a week or less during a year. Harvesting them can only be done by hand, and the time of day can have a significant impact on the amount of flavor in the flowers. But when done right, the flavor can be otherworldly—a whole different way to enjoy the bouquet of a flower . . . or a wine.

The best time to pick blossoms and herbs is between mid-morning and early afternoon, after the sun has lifted the dew but before it has evaporated the floral essence. Keep in mind that plants use their scent to attract bees and other beneficial creatures during this time of day; blossoms gathered during hot and late afternoons may have less flavor. When picking, put the blossoms or herbs in an open paper bag so they can continue to breathe. Putting them in sealed plastic containers will cause them to sweat and turn into mush.

If fresh blossoms and herbs are not available, dried ones work nearly as well. Generally, use about 2 ounces of dried flowers or herbs per gallon.

Strong Waters

Angelica

JESUIT MISSIONARIES BROUGHT what became known as Mission variety grapes from Spain to California in the mid-sixteenth century. At one time, it was the most planted grape in the state. Though the grape isn't grown much anymore, Angelica, a blend of brandy and Mission grape juice, is still made by some boutique wineries.

When making a batch of red wine, set aside a pint or two of the unfermented juice for a batch of Angelica. Bottle the juice half and half with brandy and let it sit for a few weeks so the ingredients can get acquainted.

> **Serving Suggestion:** Serve at room temperature in a port glass.

Dandelion Wine

THIS WINE IS traditionally started on April 23, St. George's Day, then served at Christmas. While you can sample a bottle earlier, it greatly benefits from aging. It can take a couple of months to clear, so it's better to let this sit in a secondary fermenter until it does before bottling.

Dandelion has a reputation as an excellent blood and liver tonic. Its benefits were documented in the tenth-century works of Arab physicians, and it was grown and used as an herb from India to Wales before we relegated it to being a weed we poison so our lawns look more uniform.

> **Note:** Use only the yellow part of the blossoms to make this wine; the sepal, or green part at the base of the blossom, is bitter enough to overpower the flavor of the rest of the blossom.

1 gallon water

7 cups (3½ pounds) sugar

1 teaspoon yeast nutrient

1 teaspoon grape tannin, or a cup of black tea

5 quarts dandelion flowers with the sepals chopped off

1 ounce ginger, peeled and sliced

Juice of 2 lemons

Juice of 1 orange

1 packet yeast: Pasteur Champagne

1 Campden tablet, crushed

½ teaspoon bentonite

1. Heat the water to a boil, add the sugar, yeast nutrient, and tannin (or tea), and stir until dissolved. Turn off the heat.
2. Put the blossoms and ginger in a nylon straining bag and put the bag into the primary fermenter.

3. Pour the hot liquid over the bag.

4. When the liquid has cooled to room temperature, stir in the lemon and orange juices, then add the yeast. Snap on the fermenter lid and attach the airlock.

5. For the next few days, slosh the fermenter around or use a sanitized spoon to flip and moisten the bag.

6. After 5 days, remove the bag from the fermenting must, squeezing it gently to extract as much liquid as possible without pressing out any of the solids. Transfer the liquid to a secondary fermenter.

7. When all fermentation has stopped, usually after another week or two, add the crushed Campden tablet. The wine should clear in 2 months. The wine has a great color, so you may want to wait for it to clear. But if you must expedite the process, add a fining agent right after the Campden tablet. Boil 1 cup of water and thoroughly mix in ½ teaspoon of bentonite. Then pour this mixture into the fermenter, attach the airlock, and swish the fermenter around to mix the fining agent into the wine.

8. When clear, bottle and age for 4 to 8 months. Be sure to save a couple of bottles for Christmas and New Year's.

Serving Suggestion: This ages into a surprisingly fine white, similar to a dry Riesling. Serve chilled with cheeses, appetizers, or seafood.

Elderflower Wine

THE FLOWERS OF the elderberry, also called *elderblow*, have been used by many cultures in teas, tonics, and wines and reportedly have many of the same benefits as the berries, alleviating the symptoms of colds and flu, as well as providing antiviral, anti-inflammatory, and antioxidant benefits.

The dried flowers are sometimes included in home winemaking kits to add color and flavor to white wines. The flowers are also featured in at least two herbal liquors: Sambuca and St. Germain.

Elder usually grows in patches at the edge of deciduous forests, or by marshes, streams, or rivers. It flowers in late spring. When picking the flowers, smell them first to make sure you like the scent. Since you don't need many blossoms to make a batch of wine, search around to find the flowers you like best.

When fresh, the flowers are white or pale yellow. If you don't use them within a few hours after picking, they can turn brown and black. It takes 2 cups of flowers to make 1 gallon of wine, and a good way to harvest them is to fill a quart jar about half full with water, then fill the rest of the jar with blossoms. You can refrigerate the jar for up to 1 week before you make the wine.

> 1 gallon water
>
> 4 cups (2 pounds) sugar
>
> 1 teaspoon yeast nutrient
>
> 1 teaspoon grape tannin, or a cup of black tea
>
> 2 cups elderflowers
>
> 1 12-ounce can frozen grape juice concentrate, thawed
>
> Juice of 2 lemons
>
> 1 packet yeast: Pasteur Champagne or Lalvin RC212
>
> 1 Campden tablet, crushed

1. Heat the water to a boil, add the sugar, yeast nutrient, and tannin (or tea), and stir until dissolved. Turn off the heat.

2. Put the flowers into a nylon straining bag. If you've stored the blossoms in a jar of water, pour the liquid through the bag so that the water is added to the boiled liquid and the blossoms remain in the bag.

3. Put the bag and grape juice concentrate in the primary fermenter and pour the hot liquid over it.

4. When the liquid has cooled to room temperature, stir in the lemon juice, then add the yeast. Snap on the fermenter lid and attach the airlock.

5. For the next few days, slosh the fermenter around or use a sanitized spoon to flip and moisten the bag.

6. After 3 days, remove the bag from the fermenting must, squeezing it gently to extract as much liquid as possible without pressing out any of the solids. Transfer the liquid to a secondary fermenter.

7. When all fermentation has stopped, usually after another week or two, add the crushed Campden tablet. Swish the fermenter around to mix it in. The wine should clear in another 2 to 3 weeks.

8. Bottle and age for at least 6 months.

Serving Suggestion: Serve chilled in a white wine glass. This wine goes nicely with dessert.

Tea Wine

USING TEA IS a simple and excellent way to make herbal wine. The ingredients are inexpensive and prepackaged, and the tea boxes normally describe any medicinal effects of the teas. And finally, it's easy to sample them as tea before committing to a batch of wine.

Teas that can produce good wines include black teas such as Orange Pekoe and Earl Grey and herbal teas such as mint and hibiscus, but be sure to experiment with your favorite flavors.

> **1 gallon water**
> **6 cups (3 pounds) sugar**
> **1 teaspoon yeast nutrient**
> **8 tea bags**
> **1 pound raisins, chopped (about 3 cups)**
> **Juice of 2 lemons**
> **1 packet yeast: Pasteur Red**
> **1 Campden tablet, crushed**
> **½ teaspoon bentonite**

1. Boil the water, add the sugar and yeast nutrient, and stir until dissolved. Add the tea bags. Turn off the heat and cover the pot. Remove the bags after 5 minutes.
2. Put the raisins in a nylon straining bag and add them to the primary fermenter. Pour the hot liquid over the bag.
3. When the liquid has cooled to room temperature, stir in the lemon juice, then add the yeast. Snap on the fermenter lid and attach the airlock.
4. For the next few days, slosh the fermenter around or use a sanitized spoon to moisten and flip the bag. This helps the yeast come into contact with more of the fruit.

5. After 10 days, remove the bag of raisins, squeezing it gently to extract as much liquid as possible without pressing out any of the solids. Transfer the liquid to a secondary fermenter.

6. When all fermentation has stopped, usually after another week or two, add the crushed Campden tablet. The wine should clear in another month or two. If the tea you used had plenty of color and tannin, feel free to use bentonite to clear it: Boil 1 cup of water and thoroughly mix in ½ teaspoon of bentonite. Then pour this mixture into the fermenter, attach the airlock, and swish the fermenter around to mix the fining agent into the wine.

7. When clear, bottle and age for at least 2 months.

Serving Suggestion: Serve chilled in a white wine glass. The food pairing depends on the tea you use; have fun experimenting.

Maple Wine

IF YOU'VE BEEN reading this book sequentially, by now you have concluded that human beings have made fermented drinks out of anything containing sugar. Now you'll see that this includes tree sap. Making wine and beer from maple sap was quite common in Colonial times, as it was one of the few native sugar sources available. (Honey bees are not native to the United States and were first imported from England in the seventeenth century. Sugarcane was not grown in the United States until the mid-eighteenth century.) Maple wine is still popular in parts of Canada.

This simple recipe makes a complex, medium-bodied white wine. After the yeast converts the sugar to alcohol, the maple syrup leaves a pleasant, woody astringency that flips traditional winemaking on its head. Winemakers typically ferment sugary grape juice and store it in wood to add astringency and vanilla tones. With maple, the fermentation removes the sweetness and reveals the inherent woody aroma. If you like rich white wines aged in wood, you have to try this.

> 3 quarts water
> 1 quart maple syrup
> 1 teaspoon acid blend
> 1 teaspoon yeast nutrient
> 1 package yeast: Pasteur Champagne or Premier Cuvée
> 1 Campden tablet, crushed
> ½ teaspoon bentonite

1. Heat the water, then stir in the syrup, acid blend, and yeast nutrient. Since maple syrup has been heat-condensed, it's already sanitized, so you don't need to boil the liquid. Just heat it until the syrup and water are well mixed.

2. Pour the liquid into the primary fermenter; when it's cooled to room temperature, add the yeast. Snap on the fermenter lid and attach the airlock.

3. Let the mixture ferment for a full month, then transfer to a secondary fermenter. You'll see a constant layer of foam on top and think that it will finish fermenting quickly. It won't. Maple syrup has a lot of sugars, but it also contains unfermentable material, so give it plenty of time to ferment and clear.

4. When all fermentation has stopped, usually another 3 or 4 weeks after it's in the secondary fermenter, add the crushed Campden tablet. This wine has a nice color, and I advise you to wait the 6 to 8 weeks it takes to clear on its own. If you're in a hurry, add a fining agent right after the Campden tablet. Boil 1 cup of water and thoroughly mix in ½ teaspoon of bentonite. Then pour this mixture into the fermenter, attach the airlock, and swish the fermenter around to mix the fining agent into the wine.

5. When clear, bottle and age for at least 4 months.

Serving suggestion: Maple wine is excellent after dinner with fruit desserts. Served slightly chilled in a white wine glass.

Rice Wine (But Not Sake)

YOU CAN OFTEN tell how advanced a culture is by noting how much time and trouble it takes to prepare its alcoholic beverages. Using that criteria, Japanese culture is light years ahead of the West.

In Japan there are more than fifteen hundred sake brewers. A particular brand can be made from any of perhaps ten strains of rice and a half dozen strains of yeast. Water is everyone's secret ingredient, of course, and the beverage can cycle through a total brewing and aging process that can take anywhere from 6 to 9 months and varies according to the skill, opinions, and school of the *toji* (sake brew master). Unlike commercial beer brewing in the United States, the time of year the sake is made and the climate also affect the final product.

The following recipe will make a beverage that will be unlike any sake consumed in Japan. How can this be? Because the steamed rice used to make sake is first inoculated with a mold called *koji*, which this recipe doesn't call for. Aside from adding a chestnut flavor, the koji mold converts much of the rice starch into sugars that the yeast can then ferment. Humility, simplicity, and common sense prevent me from covering the complicated process for making sake. That said, this recipe *is* a kind of rice wine.

> 1 gallon water
>
> 4 cups (2 pounds) sugar
>
> 2 teaspoons acid blend
>
> 1 teaspoon yeast nutrient
>
> 5 cups (2½ pounds) polished rice
>
> 1 pound golden raisins, chopped (3 cups)
>
> ½ teaspoon pectin enzyme
>
> 1 packet yeast: Wyeast Sake #9 or Flor Sherry
>
> 1 Campden tablet, crushed
>
> ½ teaspoon bentonite

1. Boil the water, add the sugar, acid blend, and yeast nutrient, and stir until dissolved. Turn off the heat.
2. Place the rice and chopped raisins in a nylon straining bag. Tie the top and place it in the boiling liquid for 10 minutes.
3. Transfer the bag to the primary fermenter, then pour in the hot liquid.
4. When the liquid has cooled to room temperature, stir in the pectin enzyme, then add the yeast. Snap on the fermenter lid and attach the airlock.
5. For the next few days, slosh the fermenter around or use a sanitized spoon to flip and moisten the bag. This helps the yeast come into contact with more of the fruit.
6. After 10 days, remove the bag, squeezing it gently to extract as much liquid as possible without pressing out any of the solids. Transfer the liquid to the secondary fermenter.
7. When all fermentation has stopped, usually after another 6 to 8 weeks, add the crushed Campden tablet. The wine will take another 1 to 2 months to clear, even with a fining agent. Boil 1 cup of water and thoroughly mix in ½ teaspoon of bentonite. Then pour this mixture into the fermenter, attach the airlock, and swish the fermenter around to mix the fining agent into the wine.
8. When clear, bottle and age for at least 4 months.

Notes:
- It's best to use polished rice to make the wine, since the protein-rich germ and husk are removed during polishing. Protein clouds a beverage; if you can decrease the amount in the ingredients, you will reduce the cloudiness of the beverage.

- Other Asian countries also use rice as the sugar source for alcoholic beverages, and most also use a mold to help convert the rice starch to something that yeast can more easily digest. Rice wine goes by various names:

  Bali: *brem*
  Borneo: *lihing, tuak*
  China: *choujiu, mijiu*
  India: *sonti*
  Korea: *cheongju, gamju, makgeolli*
  Thailand: *sato*
  Tibet: *raksi*
  Vietnam: *ruou de*

Serving Suggestion: Serve as you would a sake.

Fortified Wine

TO FORTIFY a wine means to add a distilled spirit, such as brandy, to a partially or completely fermented beverage. Port is the best known example of this. Grape must is fermented until it reaches about 7 percent alcohol, then brandy is added. This stops the yeast from fermenting the remaining sugar and raises the final alcohol level to 20 percent. The resulting beverage is both sweet, from the unfermented sugar in the wine, and strong, from the distilled spirits.

Other examples of fortified wines include Madeira, Marsala, sherry, vermouth, and the less well-heeled but still much adored MD 20/20, Thunderbird, and Wild Irish Rose. Commercial makers of fortified wines use 150 proof distilled spirits (about 75 percent alcohol), which is difficult to find or illegal to buy in some states. I usually use 100 proof spirits, which are about 50 percent alcohol.

When making wine, I often siphon off a quart to fortify. If it's a white wine, I'll add 100 proof vodka rather than brandy. Here's the process:

1. When starting a batch of wine, take a hydrometer reading and write down the potential alcohol level. For this example, let's say the potential alcohol level is 12 percent.
2. Ferment the wine as usual. After 1 week, siphon 1 quart of the still-fermenting liquid into a sanitized canning jar, screw the lid on loosely, and put it in the refrigerator. The lid should be very loose because the liquid will continue to ferment until it is cold.
3. In a week, the fermentation will have stopped, and the yeast will have settled to the bottom. At this point, remove the jar from the refrigerator and pour the clear liquid into another clean jar.
4. When the liquid gets close to room temperature but before it starts fermenting again, use your hydrometer a second time to determine the potential alcohol level. To continue the example, say the potential alcohol level is now 5 percent. This means the liquid is 7 percent alcohol (12 − 5 = 7).

MISCELLANEOUS WINES

5. Use the chart below to determine how much brandy or vodka to add so that the final alcohol level is 20 percent. First locate the correct row for the initial alcohol level of your beverage. Then multiply the volume of your beverage by the given proportion, which will give the volume of spirits that you should add. To complete the example, since you have 32 ounces of 7 percent wine, you would need to add 14 ounces of 100 proof brandy or vodka (32 x 0.43 = 13.8) to make it 20 percent.

IF YOUR BEVERAGE IS THIS % ALCOHOL	ADD THIS PROPORTION OF 100 PROOF SPIRIT
20	0
19	0.03
18	0.07
17	0.1
16	0.13
15	0.17
14	0.2
13	0.23
12	0.27
11	0.3
10	0.33
9	0.37
8	0.4
7	0.43
6	0.47
5	0.5
4	0.53
3	0.57
2	0.6
1	0.63
0	0.67

Strong Waters

6. Taste the fortified wine and add sugar to get it to the level of sweetness you want.

Notes:

- If you don't add enough distilled spirit to the wine to reach a 20 percent alcohol level, the beverage could start fermenting again. To be on the safe side, store your fortified wines in lightly corked bottles for a few weeks. If the corks pop out, the beverage is still fermenting and you need to add more distilled spirits.
- The values in the chart above were calculated using Pearson's Square, which is included at the end of this book on page 222. If you want to adjust the final alcohol level of your beverage to something other than 20 percent or use a spirit with a proof other than 100, use the square to calculate the quantities.

Serving Suggestion: Serve at room temperature in a port glass with desserts.

Soma

Hence sprinkle forth the juice effused. Soma, the
  best of sacred gifts,
Who, friend of man, hath run amid the water-
  streams. He hath pressed Soma out with stones.
Now, being purified, flow hither through the fleece
  inviolate and most odorous.
We ladden thee in waters when thou art effused,
  blending thee still with juice and milk.
Pressed out for all to see, delighting Gods, Indu,
  Far-sighted One, is mental power.
Cleansing thee, Soma, in thy stream, thou flowest
  in a watery robe:
Giver of wealth, thou sittest in the place of Law, O
  God, a fountain made of gold.
Milking the heavenly udder for dear meath, he
  hath sat in the ancient gathering place.
Washed by the men, the Strong Farseeing One
  streams forth nutritious food that all desire.
—*Rig-Veda Hymn CVII. Soma Pavamana.*

I KNOW WHAT you're thinking: *What kind of drink is a sacred gift of the gods, gives wealth, sits in the place of Law, and is, indeed, heaven's own milk? Why the hell are we getting stupid on lager and not smarter with soma?* It's a fantastic question.

The Rig-Veda, the source of this hymn to soma, is the primary religious text for Hindus. Some believe it was written by God and that it is the most ancient scripture in the world, perhaps seven thousand years old. This would make it older than the Old Testament by thousands of years.

Strangely—and I say this because there are hundreds of hymns in the Rig-Veda praising soma—there is no known recipe for it. The ingredients included the juice of a milkweedlike vine (*Asclepias acida*), barley meal, rice, clarified butter, and water. One of the other ingredients may have been the poisonous but psychedelic fly agaric mushroom (*Amanita muscaria*), or it may have been ephedra, which has been used in Oriental medicine for at least five thousand years. But no one knows. I'm including this reference to soma because it's astonishing that no one in the world now makes what was once one of the oldest and most prized drinks God ever gave us. One more reason why we should approach those nearly lost recipes with an open mind.

Meads

**Truly the righteous verily are in delight,
On couches, gazing,
Thou wilt know in their faces the radiance of
   delight.
They are given to drink of pure mead, sealed,
Whose seal is musk.**
—*The Quran 083.022–083.026*

HONEY, THAT AMBER soul-juice of a region's flora, is the ferment-able base for mead. In many parts of the ancient world, honey was the only ready source of sugar and hence the primary source of alcoholic beverages. What we call mead was known as *madhu* in Sanskrit, *methy* in Greek, and *metu* in old German. The similarity of the words indicates that the drink is older than any of these languages—meaning it's mighty old.

Mead was the ubiquitous drink of the holy throughout the ancient world: The seven-thousand-year-old Hindu text known as the Rig–Veda describes paradise as having a spring of mead; Zeus and his fellow Greek gods drank this nectar; the Norse god Odin sustained himself on the drink; Christians used mead to toast the Archangel Michael. The Celts of England drank vast quantities of the beverage and called their island home the Honey Isle of Beli.

Because of its antiquity and association with the divine, mead acquired a magical reputation in our mythologies. It was the giver of knowledge and poetry, health and immortality, and sex. The term *honeymoon* refers to the custom of drinking this honey-based beverage for a month (moon) after the wedding. Guests at ancient Moorish weddings reportedly drank honey wines to fuel their post-ceremony orgies.

As technology evolved, mead making became so specialized that its commercial production was restricted to members of a special guild. Over the centuries, however, widespread increase in barley and grape production meant that beer and wine became much less expensive to produce than mead. As this trend continued, mead consumption, once commonplace, was relegated to special occasions and eventually was reserved for only religious or state events. Currently it's available commercially only as a novelty item and is produced by a scattering of devotees.

Types of Mead

In its purest form, sometimes referred to as *show mead*, this beverage is made from honey, water, and yeast, often one part honey to four parts water. There are, however, many additions to this simple formula, which produced beverages that were common enough in ages past to have earned their own names:

- *Metheglin* is mead made with herbs or spices, such as cloves or cinnamon. Metheglin's name derives from *mead of the glen*, which, some have argued, has evolved into our word *medicine*.
- *Rhodomel* is metheglin made with roses and honey.
- *Zythos,* or *braggot,* is mead fortified with malt. One might also think of this drink as beer fortified with honey.
- *Melomel* is mead with added fruit or fruit juice.
- *Cyser* is melomel made with apples or apple juice. You could also think of this as a cider fortified with honey.
- *Morath* is melomel made with mulberries or mulberry juice.
- *Pyment* is frequently defined as a melomel made with grapes or grape juice and often herbs and spices. You could also say that pyment is wine fortified with honey.

The strength of mead is another attribute apparent in its various names:

- *Quick*, *small*, *weak*, or *short mead* is made with less honey—often five to nine parts water to one part honey—and therefore has less alcohol.
- *Tall*, *strong*, or *sack mead* is made with more honey—often three parts water to one part honey—and therefore has more alcohol and is sometimes sweeter. Some recipes advise aging this type of mead for several decades.

The amount of effervescence adds a third attribute:

- *Still mead* is flat; in other words, it has no effervescence.
- *Sparkling mead* has bubbles.

Strong Waters

Working with Honey

Meads are the most challenging beverage type in this book. Bees make honey so that it will keep indefinitely without being consumed by yeast or bacteria. You should try some of the other beverage types first, and then after you've made ciders, beers, and wines, give mead a try. Using honey adds another flavor dimension to any beverage, and many meads age as well or better than even heavy red wine.

Before it finishes fermenting, the honey-water mixture is, as in winemaking, called must. Most mead makers simmer this honey-water mixture. Not only does the honey dissolve better in hot water, but the heat also sanitizes the must. Be aware that since honey is heavier than water, it will sink in a pot of water. If you have the pot on a hot burner and don't stir occasionally, the honey will sink, stick to the bottom, and caramelize. You also need to be careful not to leave the mixture unattended while cooking, as it will boil over and make a spectacularly sticky mess of your stove.

Older recipes for making mead advise boiling the mixture for hours and skimming off the foam. This foam contains nasties that can contribute to hangovers and affect the flavor and clarity of the finished mead. The trade-off is that the longer cooking time also tends to drive off the floral aromas in the honey. I split the difference and simmer the honey for a few minutes.

Rather than heat the must to sanitize it, you could add sulfites to the liquid. Normally 1 Campden tablet will sanitize 1 gallon, and you would add the tablet 24 hours before the yeast. For the novice mead maker, heating is probably easier than adding sulfites, especially since honey dissolves nicely in hot water.

Adding Acid

Yeast works better in a slightly more acidic environment than results from simply mixing honey into water. A higher-acid environment also helps prevent other microorganisms from growing. Adding fruit juice to a honey-water mixture is one good way to boost acidity.

Adding Yeast Nutrient

Honey is low in some of the nutrients that yeast require to live. Herbs and fruit juices may contribute the missing nutrients, but you can also add a powdered yeast nutrient, which is available from winemaking supply shops.

Fermentation

Mead will take longer to ferment than beer or wine—sometimes much longer. This means that while the initial fermentation may be vigorous, the beverage may not finish for a month or three, so adjust your expectations accordingly.

Standard Mead

THIS RECIPE MAKES what is sometimes called *show mead*. It's a pure product that accentuates the flavor of the honey and yields a drink that's about 10 percent alcohol.

> **3 quarts water**
>
> **3⅓ cups (2½ pounds) wildflower honey**
>
> **1 teaspoon acid blend**
>
> **1 teaspoon yeast nutrient**
>
> **1 packet yeast: Pasteur Champagne or Premier Cuvée**
>
> **1 Campden tablet, crushed**
>
> **½ teaspoon bentonite**

1. Heat the water and stir in the honey, acid blend, and yeast nutrient. Note that honey is heavier than water and will tend to sink to the bottom and burn if you don't mix it in well. Simmer, but do not boil, for 10 minutes. If foam rises to the top, skim it off and discard. If the foam is brown, skim it off, discard, and turn down the heat. Pour the hot liquid into the primary fermenter.

2. When the liquid has cooled to room temperature, add the yeast. Snap on the fermenter lid and attach the airlock.

3. After 2 weeks, transfer the liquid to the secondary fermenter . . . and wait. Mead can take a month or two to finish fermenting.

4. Once every week, observe the fermenter. When you don't see a bubble for at least 2 minutes, you can assume that the fermentation is essentially finished.

5. Add the crushed Campden tablet. At this point, the mead should clear in another 2 to 3 weeks. To expedite the process, add a fining agent right after the Campden tablet. Boil 1 cup of water and thoroughly mix in ½ teaspoon of bentonite. Then pour this mixture into the fermenter, attach the airlock, and swish the fermenter around to mix the fining agent into the mead.

6. When clear, bottle and age for at least 3 months.

Serving Suggestion: Serve lightly chilled in a white wine glass.

Small Mead

IN THIS INSTANCE, "SMALL" means a lower alcohol percentage. The goal of this recipe is to provide a sweet but refreshing beverage in a short time.

> **Zest of 1 orange**
> **½ ounce ginger, peeled and sliced**
> **3 whole cloves, cracked**
> **2 sticks cinnamon**
> **3½ quarts water**
> **2 cups (1½ pounds) wildflower honey**
> **1 teaspoon yeast nutrient**
> **1 teaspoon acid blend**
> **1 packet yeast: Pasteur Champagne or Premier Cuvée**

1. Put the zest, ginger, cloves, and cinnamon in a nylon straining bag.
2. Heat the water and stir in the honey, yeast nutrient, and acid blend. Add the bag to the liquid. Note that honey is heavier than water and will tend to sink to the bottom and burn if you don't mix it in well. Simmer, but do not boil, for 20 minutes. If foam rises to the top, skim it off and discard. If the foam is brown, skim it, discard, and turn down the heat. Pour the hot liquid, including the bag, into the primary fermenter.
3. When the liquid has cooled to room temperature, add the yeast, snap on the fermenter lid, and attach the airlock.
4. For the next few days, slosh the fermenter around or use a sanitized spoon to flip and moisten the bag.
5. After 1 week, remove the spice bag, squeezing it gently to extract as much liquid as possible without pressing out any of the solids.

6. Let the liquid ferment for 2 more weeks. As stated previously, the goal here is a light, sweet beverage, so even if it hasn't finished fermenting, bottle and refrigerate. After 1 week in the refrigerator, the yeast will have dropped to the bottom of the bottles and the beverage will be ready to drink.

Note: Because this beverage won't ferment to completion in 3 weeks, you may want to consider bottling it in plastic soda bottles. For the same reason, you should refrigerate the bottles; don't leave them out for more than a few hours, as they may pop.

Serving Suggestion: Serve lightly chilled in a white wine glass.

CIDER, WHILE A fine drink, becomes a classic when it has enough alcohol to preserve it for a few years. And though you can add sugar to cider to make an apple wine, it's the mating of honey with cider that creates a time-tested cyser.

> 1 quart water
>
> 2 cups (1½ pounds) orange blossom honey
>
> 1 teaspoon acid blend
>
> 1 teaspoon yeast nutrient
>
> ½ teaspoon grape tannin, or a cup of black tea
>
> 2 quarts apple juice
>
> ½ teaspoon pectin enzyme, if using unfiltered juice
>
> 1 packet yeast: Pasteur Champagne
>
> 1 Campden tablet, crushed
>
> ½ teaspoon bentonite

1. Heat the water and stir in the honey, acid blend, yeast nutrient, and tannin (or tea). Note that honey is heavier than water and will tend to sink to the bottom and burn if you don't mix it in well. Simmer, but do not boil, for 5 minutes. If foam rises to the top, skim it off and discard. If the foam is brown, skim it, discard, and turn down the heat. Pour the hot liquid into the primary fermenter.

2. When the liquid has cooled to room temperature, stir in the apple juice and pectin enzyme, then add the yeast. Snap on the fermenter lid and attach the airlock.

3. After 2 weeks, transfer the beverage to a secondary fermenter.

4. Once a week, observe the fermenter. Cyser can take a month or two to finish fermenting. When you don't see a bubble for at least 2 minutes, its fermentation is essentially finished.

5. Add the crushed Campden tablet. At this point, the mead should clear in another 2 to 3 weeks. To expedite the process, add a fining agent right after the Campden tablet. Boil 1 cup of water and thoroughly mix in ½ teaspoon of bentonite. Then pour this mixture into the fermenter, attach the airlock, and swish the fermenter around to mix the fining agent into the mead.

6. When clear, bottle and age for at least 3 months.

Note: Apple juice contains a lot of pectin. Adding it to the simmering honey mixture may result in a cloudy beverage. Be sure to wait until the mixture cools before adding the apple juice and pectin enzyme.

Serving Suggestion: Serve lightly chilled in a white wine glass with shellfish.

Metheglin

A Cossack is not born to run around after women. You would like to hide [your sons] under your petticoat, and sit upon them as a hen sits on eggs. Go, go, and let us have everything there is on the table in a trice. We don't want any dumplings, honey-cakes, poppy-cakes, or any other such messes: give us a whole sheep, a goat, mead forty years old, and as much corn-brandy as possible, not with raisins and all sorts of stuff, but plain scorching corn-brandy, which foams and hisses like mad.

—*Nikolai Vasilievich Gogol,* Taras Bulba

WHEN YOU CONSIDER that Cossacks were a wild, seminomadic people, the idea that they would go to the trouble to age a honey wine for 40 years says something about the value that many placed on the beverage.

You can produce a huge variety of flavors and effects when mixing herbs and spices for a metheglin. These types of meads benefit the most by aging. Here's a standard recipe that produces a healthful drink guaranteed to make a blind man hear and a deaf man see. If you make a gallon batch, try drinking a bottle every 3 months and recording your impressions. At 3 months, you may not be impressed, but by the time you try the last bottle, a year later, you'll have some understanding of what aging can do for a metheglin. As shown by the intro quote for this recipe, it's not uncommon to find recipes or references in literature to recipes that are aged for decades before they are enjoyed. If you develop a metheglin recipe you especially like, you might want to set part of a batch aside for the distant future.

2 nutmegs, quartered

2 cinnamon sticks

1 ounce ginger, peeled and sliced

10 whole cloves, cracked

3 quarts water

3 ⅓ cups (2 ½ pounds) honey: sage, mesquite, or wildflower

1 teaspoon yeast nutrient

1 teaspoon acid blend

½ teaspoon grape tannin, or a cup of black tea

1 packet yeast: Pasteur Champagne or Premier Cuvée

1 Campden tablet, crushed

½ teaspoon bentonite

1. Put the nutmeg, cinnamon, ginger, and cloves in a nylon straining bag.

2. Heat the water and stir in the honey, yeast nutrient, acid blend, and tannin (or tea). (Sage honey is the best for this recipe.) Add the bag to the liquid. Note that honey is heavier than water and will tend to sink to the bottom and burn if you don't mix it in well. Simmer, but do not boil, for 20 minutes. If foam rises to the top, skim it off and discard. If the foam is brown, skim it, discard, and turn down the heat. Pour the hot liquid into the primary fermenter.

3. When the liquid has cooled to room temperature, add the yeast, snap on the fermenter lid, and attach the airlock.

4. For the next few days, slosh the fermenter around or use a sanitized spoon to flip and moisten the bag.

5. After 2 weeks, remove the spice bag, squeezing it gently to extract as much liquid as possible without pressing out any of the solids. Transfer the liquid to a secondary fermenter.

6. Once a week, observe the fermenter. Metheglin can take a month or two to finish fermenting. When you don't see a bubble for at least 2 minutes, you can assume its fermentation is essentially finished.

7. Add the crushed Campden tablet. At this point, the metheglin should clear in another 2 to 3 weeks. To expedite the process, add a fining agent right after the Campden tablet. Boil 1 cup of water and thoroughly mix in ½ teaspoon of bentonite. Then pour this mixture into the fermenter, attach the airlock, and swish the fermenter around to mix the fining agent into the liquid.

8. When clear, bottle and age for at least 6 months. This beverage improves over time, so be sure to save a bottle.

Serving Suggestion: Try this metheglin as a post-dinner digestif. Serve lightly chilled in a white wine glass.

Mint Metheglin

MINT HELPS DIGESTION, so this metheglin makes an excellent after-dinner drink. It also makes an interesting alternative to mint juleps on Kentucky Derby day. Peppermint is most often used for metheglins, but spearmint is also refreshing.

2 ounces ginger, peeled and sliced

4 cups fresh mint leaves

3 quarts water

3 1/3 cups (2 1/2 pounds) honey: orange blossom or clover

1 teaspoon yeast nutrient

1 teaspoon acid blend

1 packet yeast: Pasteur Champagne or Premier Cuvée

1 Campden tablet, crushed

1/2 teaspoon bentonite

1. Put the ginger and mint in a nylon straining bag.
2. Heat the water and stir in the honey, yeast nutrient, and acid blend. Add the bag with the ginger and mint. Note that honey is heavier than water and will tend to sink to the bottom and burn if you don't mix it in well. Simmer the liquid just long enough to mix the honey and water thoroughly. If foam rises to the top, skim it off and discard. If the foam is brown, skim it, discard, and turn down the heat. Pour the hot liquid into the primary fermenter.
3. When the liquid has cooled to room temperature, add the yeast, snap on the fermenter lid, and attach the airlock.
4. For the next few days, slosh the fermenter around or use a sanitized spoon to flip and moisten the bag.
5. After 1 week, remove the bag, squeezing it gently to extract as much liquid as possible without pressing out any of the solids. Transfer the liquid to a secondary fermenter.

6. Once a week, observe the fermenter. Metheglin can take a month or two to finish fermenting. When you don't see a bubble for at least 2 minutes, its fermentation is essentially finished.

7. Add the crushed Campden tablet. At this point, the metheglin should clear in another 2 to 3 weeks. Avoid using a fining agent to clear this beverage, as the mint flavor is delicate.

8. When clear, bottle and age for at least 6 months.

Serving Suggestion: Try serving this as an aperitif, lightly chilled.

Rhodomel

THE ANCIENT GREEKS made this beverage from roses and honey. Can any drink be more romantic?

The main challenge with using any delicately flavored herb or flower in a fermented beverage is to prevent the bubbling action of the fermentation from driving off the aromas. This ingenious recipe reduces the loss by adding the rose petals late in the fermentation. You can also use a neutral-flavored honey, a pasteurized clover honey for example, to help keep the focus on the roses.

It's best to collect petals from newly opened roses. Pull the petals from the sepal, the green section at the base of the bud. If you don't have rose bushes yourself, find someone who does and offer to split a batch of rhodomel with them in exchange for the petals. If you can't get enough petals for a batch in one picking, freeze them until you can collect more.

3 quarts water

3⅓ cups (2½ pounds) clover honey

1 teaspoon acid blend

1 teaspoon yeast nutrient

½ teaspoon grape tannin, or a cup of black tea

1 packet yeast: Pasteur Champagne

12 cups rose petals

1 Campden tablet, crushed

1. Heat the water and stir in the honey, acid blend, yeast nutrient, and tannin (or tea). Note that honey is heavier than water and will tend to sink to the bottom and burn if you don't mix it in well. Simmer, but do not boil, for 5 minutes. If foam rises to the top, skim it off and discard. If the foam is brown, skim it, discard, and turn down the heat. Pour the liquid into the primary fermenter.

2. When the liquid has cooled to room temperature, add the yeast, snap on the fermenter lid, and attach the airlock.
3. One week after fermentation starts, put the rose petals in a nylon straining bag and submerge it in the primary fermenter.
4. For the next few days, slosh the fermenter around or use a sanitized spoon to flip and moisten the bag.
5. After another 10 days, remove the bag of petals, squeezing it gently to extract as much liquid as possible without pressing out any of the solids. Transfer the liquid to a secondary fermenter.
6. Once every week or two, observe the fermenter. Rhodomel can take a month or two to finish fermenting. When you don't see a bubble for at least 2 minutes, its fermentation is essentially finished.
7. Add the crushed Campden tablet. At this point, the rhodomel should clear in another 4 or 5 weeks. Because of the delicate bouquet of this beverage, I don't advise using a fining agent to help it clear faster.
8. When clear, bottle and age for at least 6 months.

Serving Suggestion: Serve rhodomel as a predinner alternative to Champagne. It's a memorable beverage to toast with. Serve lightly chilled in a white wine glass.

Pyment

He wooeth her by means and by brocage,
And swore he woulde be her owen page.
He singeth brokking as a nightingale.
He sent her piment, mead, and spiced ale,
And wafers piping hot out of the glede.
—*Geoffrey Chaucer,* **The Canterbury Tales, "The Miller's Tale"**

BY THE MIDDLE AGES, grape cultivation and the expanding wine industry had diluted England's historic attachment to honey-based beverages. However, as the writings of the time prove, meads were still preferred over wine and ordinary beer. Pyment, a beverage made from grapes and honey (and once spelled *piment*), was a much-appreciated exotic. It was also rumored to be an aphrodisiac.

As you might imagine, when making a pyment, the ratio of grapes to honey varies from recipe to recipe. Since all of us are more familiar with the taste of grape- rather than honey-based wine, this recipe reflects that modern preference. The procedure also takes a bit more effort than making either a wine or a mead. But when you're wooing a maiden, what's a little extra effort?

> **2 quarts water**
> **1⅓ cups (1 pound) honey: clover or orange blossom**
> **6 pounds grapes**
> **1 packet yeast: Pasteur Champagne or Pasteur Red**
> **2 Campden tablets, crushed**
> **1 teaspoon bentonite**

1. Heat the water and stir in the honey. Note that honey is heavier than water and will tend to sink to the bottom and burn if you don't mix it in well. Simmer, but do not boil, for 5 minutes, or until thoroughly mixed. If foam rises to the top, skim it off and discard. If the foam is brown, skim it, discard, and turn down the heat.

2. Turn off the heat and let the liquid cool to room temperature. (Adding hot liquid to the grape juice could cause the pectins in the grapes to cloud the beverage.)

3. Meanwhile, de-stem the grapes, put them in the primary fermenter, and crush with your hands or a potato masher. Don't use a food processor because the blades will cut the seeds and make the wine bitter.

4. Add one of the crushed Campden tablets to the juice and fruit. Pour the cooled honey mixture into the primary fermenter. Cover the fermenter with the lid.

5. Wait 24 hours, then add the yeast, snap on the fermenter lid, and attach the airlock.

6. For the next few days, slosh the fermenter around or use a sanitized spoon to break up the fruit cap. This helps the yeast come into contact with more of the grapes.

7. Ten days after fermentation begins, separate the fermenting must from the fruit. You can use a sanitized colander to scoop out the floating cap. The remaining solids will eventually sink to the bottom. Transfer the liquid to a secondary fermenter.

8. Wait until all fermentation has stopped. Since this mixture has honey in it, fermentation could take several more weeks to finish. Have patience.

9. Add the second crushed Campden tablet. At this point, the pyment should clear in another 2 to 3 weeks. To expedite the process, add a fining agent right after the Campden tablet. Boil 1 cup of water and thoroughly mix in 1 teaspoon of bentonite. Then pour this mixture into the fermenter, attach the airlock, and swish the fermenter around to mix the fining agent into the liquid.

10. When clear, bottle and age for at least 6 months.

Serving Suggestion: Serve as you would a rosé, lightly chilled in a white wine glass. Try it with fruit desserts.

Blackberry Melomel

BLACKBERRIES HAVE TRADITIONALLY been prescribed for sore throats, digestive problems, hemorrhoids, and all parts in between. The berries are loaded with antioxidants and nutrients such as vitamins C and E, folate, potassium, manganese, and other good stuff.

These berries grow wild in many parts of the country, and during the summer, it's fairly easy to gather a few pounds. If you can't gather enough in one picking to warrant a batch of melomel, just freeze them until you have enough. Of course, you can also buy them frozen. Frozen berries are just as good as fresh ones when used to make this melomel.

This is my favorite melomel to make. Every batch is different. You don't need to add acid and tannin when using blackberries; they contain enough of their own to make a great beverage. The easiest way to process a few pounds is to squish them with your hands while the berries are in a nylon straining bag in the primary fermenter.

3 quarts water

3 ⅓ cups (2½ pounds) honey: clover or orange blossom

1 teaspoon yeast nutrient

3 pounds blackberries (9 cups)

½ teaspoon pectin enzyme

1 packet yeast: Pasteur Champagne or Wyeast Dry Mead

1 Campden tablet, crushed

½ teaspoon bentonite

1. Heat the water and stir in the honey and yeast nutrient. Note that honey is heavier than water and will tend to sink to the bottom and burn if you don't mix it in well. Simmer, but do not boil, for 10 minutes, or until the honey totally dissolves. If foam rises to the top, skim it off and discard. If the foam is brown, skim it, discard, and turn down the heat.

2. Put the blackberries in a nylon straining bag, place it in the primary fermenter, and squish it with your hands. Since black-berries contain pectin, don't pour the liquid on them when it's still boiling. Give the hot honey mixture 10 minutes to cool before pouring it on the berries.

3. When the liquid has cooled to room temperature, stir in the pectin enzyme and add the yeast. Then snap on the fermenter lid and attach the airlock.

4. For the next few days, slosh the fermenter around or use a sanitized spoon to flip and moisten the bag. This helps the yeast come into contact with more of the berries.

5. Ten days after fermentation begins, remove the bag of fruit from the fermenting must, squeezing it gently to extract as much liquid as possible without pressing out any of the solids. Transfer the liquid to a secondary fermenter. Any remaining solids in the beverage will eventually sink.

6. Wait until all fermentation has stopped. Because this mixture has honey in it, this could take several more weeks. Once a week, observe the fermenter. When you don't see a bubble for at least 2 minutes, its fermentation is essentially finished.

7. Add the crushed Campden tablet. The melomel should clear in another 2 to 3 weeks. To expedite the process, add a fining agent right after the Campden tablet. Boil 1 cup of water and thoroughly mix in ½ teaspoon of bentonite. Then pour this mixture into the fermenter, attach the airlock, and swish the fermenter around to mix the fining agent into the liquid.

8. When clear, bottle and age for at least 6 months.

Serving Suggestion: This goes great with chocolate desserts. Serve at room temperature or lightly chilled in a red wine glass.

Strawberry Melomel

STRAWBERRIES AND HONEY sound like ingredients for a dessert, but when mixed and fermented, they become a heady, dry, and aromatic drink.

I've served this melomel many times. Although few can identify the fruit by tasting the beverage, the scent of strawberries fills the air in a few hours if you set a glass of this down in a room, at which point most people look for the bowl of strawberries.

3 quarts water

3⅓ cups (2½ pounds) honey: clover or orange blossom

1 teaspoon yeast nutrient

½ teaspoon grape tannin, or a cup of black tea

3 pounds strawberries (9 cups)

1 packet yeast: Pasteur Champagne or Wyeast Dry Mead

1 Campden tablet, crushed

1. Heat the water and stir in the honey, yeast nutrient, and tannin (or tea). Note that honey is heavier than water and will tend to sink to the bottom and burn if you don't mix it in well. Simmer, but do not boil, for 10 minutes. If foam rises to the top, skim it off and discard. If the foam is brown, skim it, discard, and turn down the heat.

2. Put the fruit into a nylon straining bag, put the bag in the primary fermenter, and squish it with your hands. Pour the hot liquid into the primary fermenter. Strawberries don't have much pectin, so there's little chance that this beverage will get hazy.

3. When the liquid has cooled to room temperature, add the yeast, snap on the fermenter lid, and attach the airlock.

4. For the next few days, slosh the fermenter around or use a sanitized spoon to flip and moisten the bag. This helps the yeast come into contact with more of the fruit.

5. Ten days after fermentation begins, remove the bag of fruit, squeezing it gently to extract as much liquid as possible without pressing out any of the solids. Transfer the liquid to a secondary fermenter. Any remaining solids in the beverage will eventually sink.

6. Wait until all fermentation has stopped. Because this mixture has honey in it, this could take several more weeks. Once a week, observe the fermenter. When you don't see a bubble for at least 2 minutes, its fermentation is essentially finished.

7. Add the crushed Campden tablet. This melomel should take another 2 to 3 weeks to clear. Because of the delicate color and bouquet of this beverage, I don't advise using a fining agent to help it clear faster.

8. When clear, bottle and age for at least 3 months.

Serving Suggestion: It may look like a rosé, but please don't chill this. Strawberry melomel is so good I recommend having it by itself, at room temperature, in a red wine glass or brandy snifter.

Morath (Mulberry Melomel)

*Oswald, broach the oldest wine-cask;
place the best mead, the mightiest ale,
the richest morath, the most sparkling
cider, the most odoriferous pigments,
upon the board; fill the largest horns.*
— *Sir Walter Scott*, Ivanhoe

ALTHOUGH PEOPLE USED to value mulberry fruit for making morath, modern homeowners regret having these fast-growing shade trees in their yards, mostly because birds love to eat the berries, which pass quickly through them and transform nearby cars into avian modern-art canvases. In fact, even without birds, the trees themselves shed enormous quantities of berries, which make any surface beneath them sticky.

You can't buy them in stores or farmers' markets, but in many parts of the country you can easily gather buckets of mulberries during the summer.

> 3 quarts water
> 3⅓ cups (2½ pounds) honey: clover, orange blossom, or
>   lemon blossom
> 1 teaspoon yeast nutrient
> ½ teaspoon grape tannin, or a cup of black tea
> 2 sticks cinnamon
> 4 pounds mulberries (12 cups)
> ½ teaspoon pectin enzyme
> 1 packet yeast: Pasteur Champagne or Wyeast Dry Mead
> ½ teaspoon bentonite

1. Heat the water and stir in the honey, yeast nutrient, and tannin (or tea). Note that honey is heavier than water and will tend to sink to the bottom and burn if you don't mix it in well. Add the

cinnamon sticks. Simmer, but do not boil, for 10 minutes. If foam rises to the top, skim it off and discard. If the foam is brown, skim it, discard, and turn down the heat. Remove the cinnamon.

2. Put the fruit into a nylon straining bag, put the bag in the primary fermenter, and squish it with your hands. Pour the hot liquid into the fermenter.

3. When the liquid has cooled to room temperature, stir in the pectin enzyme, then add the yeast. Snap on the fermenter lid and attach the airlock.

4. For the next few days, slosh the fermenter around or use a sanitized spoon to flip and moisten the bag. This helps the yeast come into contact with more of the berries.

5. Five days after fermentation begins, remove the bag, squeezing it gently to extract as much liquid as possible without pressing out any of the solids. Transfer the liquid to a secondary fermenter. Any remaining solids in the beverage will eventually sink.

6. Wait until all fermentation has stopped. Because this mixture has honey in it, this could take several more weeks. Once a week, observe the fermenter. When you don't see a bubble for at least 2 minutes, its fermentation is essentially finished.

7. Add the crushed Campden tablet. The melomel should clear in another 2 to 3 weeks. To expedite the process, add a fining agent right after the Campden tablet. Boil 1 cup of water and thoroughly mix in ½ teaspoon of bentonite. Then pour this mixture into the fermenter, attach the airlock, and swish the fermenter around to mix the fining agent into the liquid.

8. When clear, bottle and age for at least 6 months.

Serving Suggestion: Serve at room temperature in a red wine glass, unless your drinking horn is handy. This medium-bodied and tart melomel is good with game meats.

Plum Melomel

How the flowers of the plum flutter and turn! Do I not think of you?
But your house is distant.
The Master said, "It is the want of thought about it. How is it distant?"
—*Confucian Analects*

WRITERS SINCE CONFUCIUS' time have celebrated plums, and the fruit has been enjoyed fresh, cooked in desserts, dried into prunes, and made into wine. Using them in a melomel can result in a luscious and gorgeous beverage.

Plums are also chock-full of antioxidants, contain minerals that help protect bones, and include phenols that help prevent the oxidation of cholesterol, which helps to protect your heart. People who have plum trees in their yards are often eager to get rid of the fruit. Offering to split a batch of plum melomel with them may yield all the plums you want.

3 quarts water

2 cups (1½ pounds) honey: orange blossom or clover

1 teaspoon yeast nutrient

½ teaspoon grape tannin, or a cup of black tea

4 pounds plums, split and pitted (about 12 cups)

½ teaspoon pectin enzyme

1 packet yeast: Pasteur Champagne

1 teaspoon bentonite

1 Campden tablet, crushed

Hints:

- Freeze the plums before using them. Freezing helps break down the cell walls in the fruit, making it easier for the yeast to get at the juice.
- This recipe also works well for apricots.

1. Heat the water and stir in the honey, yeast nutrient, and tannin (or tea). Note that honey is heavier than water and will tend to sink to the bottom and burn if you don't mix it in well. Simmer, but do not boil, for 5 minutes. If foam rises to the top, skim it off and discard. If the foam is brown, skim it, discard, and turn down the heat.

2. Put the fruit into a nylon straining bag, place it in the primary fermenter, and squish it with your hands. Pour the hot liquid into the primary fermenter.

3. When the liquid has cooled to room temperature, stir in the pectin enzyme and add the yeast. Snap on the fermenter lid and attach the airlock.

4. For the next few days, slosh the fermenter around or use a sanitized spoon to flip and moisten the bag. This helps the yeast come into contact with more of the fruit.

5. After 10 days, remove the bag of fruit, squeezing it gently to extract as much liquid as possible without pressing out any solids. Transfer the liquid to the secondary fermenter. Since there are a lot of fruit particles in this melomel, you can add a fining agent at this stage. Boil 1 cup of water and thoroughly mix in ½ teaspoon of bentonite. Then pour this mixture into the fermenter, attach the airlock, and swish the fermenter around to mix the fining agent into the liquid.

6. Melomel can take a month or two to finish fermenting. Once every week or two, observe the fermenter. When you don't see a bubble for at least 2 minutes, its fermentation is essentially finished.

7. Add the crushed Campden tablet. At this point, the melomel should clear in another 2 to 3 weeks. To expedite the process, add additional fining agent right after the Campden tablet. Boil 1 cup of water and thoroughly mix in ½ teaspoon of bentonite. Then pour this mixture into the fermenter, attach the airlock, and swish the fermenter around to mix the fining agent into the liquid.

8. When clear, bottle and age for at least 6 months.

Serving Suggestion: This melomel goes well with seafood and Japanese food. Serve chilled in a white wine glass.

Zythos or Braggot

SOME OF THE first written descriptions of northern Celtic and Germanic peoples describe their drinking practices. These Greek and Roman authors suggest that beverages made with malt and honey were commonly consumed by locals, who often drank them to stupefaction.

Zythos and *braggot* are terms for essentially the same drink—a mixture of mead and beer. While today there are a few tasty commercial "honey beers" available, they include honey as an accent to the malt, not as a full-blown partner, as zythos and braggot do.

To make a simple and easy zythos or braggot of your own, start off with a prehopped can of malt. These often come in 3¾-pound cans. Their instructions suggest that you add 2 pounds of sugar to the contents to make a wort that will ferment to yield a total of 6 gallons of 3.5 percent alcohol beer. Rather than add the sugar and call it a beer, instead add 2½ pounds of honey and make a zythos. Buckwheat honey adds a nutty flavor.

Note that honey takes longer to ferment than malt, so have patience before you bottle. Wait until you see no bubbles coming out of the airlock for a full 5 minutes, not the usual 2 minutes called for in most other honey-based recipes. Because you're going to carbonate the beverage with a specific amount of corn sugar, if there is residual honey as well the bottles could overcarbonate.

Aside from adding honey rather than sugar and waiting longer to bottle, follow the directions that come with the can of malt.

Strong Waters

Hard Ciders and Perry

FORGET ORANGE JUICE—hard cider is the original breakfast drink. President John Adams used to drink a quart of it before starting his busy day, and I'm sure it made him not only more agreeable, but probably as regular as a Swiss watch too.

Ciders are the easiest type of beverage to make in this book. You can buy pasteurized apple juice, add yeast, and in a week produce an acceptable dry beverage. But making a *great* hard cider from apples is a challenge; arguably even more challenging than making a fine wine.

What's so hard about making a great hard cider from apples? Just as there are particular grape varieties that are blended to create fine wine, species of apples were bred as hard cider ingredients. But unlike wine, where winemakers focus on one type of grape and add small amounts of others as an accent, cider makers routinely mix several varieties of apple juice to make a great hard cider. Most, then, are blends.

For the purposes of hard cider, apples can be divided into four categories:

- **Sweet apples** Sweet apples are high in sugar and low in acid. Varieties include Red Delicious, Cortland, Rome Beauty, and York Imperial. These constitute 25 to 50 percent of a hard cider.
- **Tart apples** Slightly acidic apples give zest to the juice. Varieties include Jonathon, Northern Spy, Winesap, and Granny Smith. These make up 25 to 40 percent of a hard cider.
- **Aromatic apples** Fragrant apples contribute to a blend's bouquet. Varieties include McIntosh, Gravenstein, Pippin, Golden Delicious, and Gala. These constitute 10 to 30 percent of a hard cider.
- **Astringent apples** Highly acidic apples also contain tannin. Varieties include crab apples and wild varieties sometimes called *spitters* for reasons that become obvious when you bite into them. These apples are used in small quantities to give the blend a unique character and also to help preserve it, since they have more tannins than other varieties. These make up less than 10 percent of a hard cider.

Juices from apples are blended to achieve a balance among acids, sugars, tannins, and aroma. Too many apples that are merely sweet will make the final hard cider bland, while too many tart apples make it overly sharp.

In the eighteenth century, when cider making was arguably at its peak, cider makers did their work in the fall. This was when apples were ripe, and perhaps more to the point, there were few other fruits available. Today we have a wide variety of juices available year-round, so we aren't restricted to using just apple juice to make a fine cider. But the flavor ratio remains much the same. In other words, choose juices according to the following profile:

- **Sweet juice** Most apple juice works well. 50 percent of the total.
- **Tart juice** Citrus juice blends serve well here. 20 to 25 percent of the total.
- **Aromatic juice** Stone fruits or berries are a good choice. 20 to 25 percent of the total.
- **Astringent juice** Cranberry is great in this role. 5 to 10 percent of the total.

Hard cider is one of those beverages in which experimentation is key in helping you develop a flavor that matches your tastes. Grocery stores stock an amazing variety of juices, and the breadth of juice types increases each year. The more cider batches you make, the better you will be able to determine what the result will be simply by tasting the juice before it ferments. In other words, you learn how to taste past the sugar in the original juice and imagine what the final beverage might taste like after the sugar has fermented.

Note: Because of concerns about salmonella, bottlers and consumers now prefer pasteurized juice. While this makes it simpler to ferment because the juice is sanitized, it also makes it more likely that cider made from unfiltered juice will be cloudy, because the heat causes the pectin in the juice to coagulate. You can use a pectin enzyme to try to clear a pasteurized unfiltered cider, but it may not work completely. Unfiltered cider from local orchards is a great base for making hard cider, though, so maybe the best option is just to accept the clouds and drink up.

Basic Hard Cider

THIS IS THE BASIC cider recipe. It's not only a great starting point to learn about making cider, it will teach you most of what you need to know about how fermentation works.

> **1 gallon pasteurized apple cider or apple juice**
> **¾ cup (6 ounces) sugar**
> **1 teaspoon yeast nutrient**
> **½ teaspoon pectin enzyme, if using unfiltered juice**
> **1 packet yeast: Premier Cuvée or Lalvin KIV-1116**
> **7 teaspoons of corn sugar, if making a sparkling cider**

1. Pour the juice into the primary fermenter. Stir in the sugar and yeast nutrient, along with the pectin enzyme if the juice is unfiltered. (Because the juice is pasteurized, you don't need to use a Campden tablet to sanitize it.)
2. Add the yeast, snap on the fermenter lid, and attach the airlock. Can this be any simpler?
3. Fermentation is usually complete in 7 to 10 days. You can bottle it as is, or if you want a sparkling cider, add 7 teaspoons of corn sugar and bottle the cider in Champagne-style bottles, beer bottles, or soda bottles. Whether you make a still or sparkling cider, you don't need to age it more than a couple of weeks, but it does become crisper after a couple of months.

Serving Suggestion: Hard cider is similar in character to a light lager and goes especially well with Spanish food or by itself. Serve cold in a pint glass.

Cranberry Cider

CRANBERRY JUICE COCKTAIL contributes a welcome tartness and astringency to this simple beverage, as well as a pleasant rose color.

> 3 quarts pasteurized apple cider or juice
>
> 1 quart cranberry juice cocktail
>
> ¾ cup (6 ounces) sugar
>
> 1 teaspoon yeast nutrient
>
> ½ teaspoon pectin enzyme, if using unfiltered juice
>
> 1 packet yeast: Premier Cuvée or Lalvin KIV-1116
>
> 7 teaspoons of corn sugar, if making a sparkling cider

1. Pour the juices into the primary fermenter. Stir in the sugar and yeast nutrient, along with the pectin enzyme if the juice is unfiltered.
2. Add the yeast, snap on the fermenter lid, and attach the airlock.
3. Fermentation is usually complete in 7 to 10 days. You can bottle it as is, or if you want a sparkling cider, add 7 teaspoons of corn sugar and bottle the cider in Champagne-style bottles, beer bottles, or soda bottles. Whether you make a still or sparkling cider, you don't need to age it more than a couple of weeks, but it does become crisper after a couple of months.

Serving Suggestion: This cider pairs well with creamy pasta sauces and cheeses. Serve cold in a pint glass.

HARD CIDERS AND PERRY

Balanced Cider

THE INGREDIENTS IN this recipe fit the flavor profile described in the introduction to this chapter: the apple juice provides the sweetness, the lemonade the tartness, the cherry juice the aroma, and the grape tannin the astringency. Try to use real juices, not "juice drinks."

This rose-colored beverage is light, dry, and flavorful and should spark some inspiration for how you might experiment with various juices to make a cider you like even better. With the variety of juices available, you can swap out ingredients in this basic recipe and develop an excellent cider of your own.

> **1 gallon filtered and pasteurized apple juice**
> **1 quart black cherry juice**
> **1 quart lemonade**
> **¼ teaspoon grape tannin, or a cup of black tea**
> **1 teaspoon yeast nutrient**
> **1 packet yeast: ale**
> **7 teaspoons of corn sugar, if making a sparkling cider**

1. Pour the juices into the primary fermenter. Stir in the yeast nutrient and tannin (or tea).
2. Add the yeast, snap on the fermenter lid, and attach the airlock.
3. Fermentation is usually complete in 7 to 10 days. You can bottle it as is, or if you want a sparkling cider, add 7 teaspoons of corn sugar and bottle the cider in Champagne-style bottles, beer bottles, or soda bottles. Whether you make a still or sparkling cider, you don't need to age it more than a couple of weeks, but it does become crisper after a couple of months.

Serving Suggestion: Serve cold in a pint glass at a summer barbecue. It's a great alternative to beer or wine; it has a taste profile similar to that of wine but with the lower alcohol level of beer.

Perry

PEARS HAVE a kind of "second city" reputation to the Big Apple. Perhaps that's undeserved. There are, after all, more than three thousand varieties of pears, about the same number as apples. In *The Odyssey*, Homer praises the fruit as a gift of the Gods. Pears store well, have a distinctive taste, and look good, if you're partial to pear-shaped fruit.

There may be fewer regions where pears thrive than apples, and the fruit tends to have less acid and tannin, but that doesn't mean that perry needs to be considered a lesser beverage than cider. Pears have more sugar than apples and more unfermentable sugar as well, so perry is naturally stronger and sweeter than cider.

Basic Perry

CHECK THE LABELS when buying pear juice. Many brands already blend pear and apple juices. If this is the case with your juice, simply use 1 gallon of the blend.

> **2 quarts apple juice**
> **2 quarts pear juice**
> **1 teaspoon yeast nutrient**
> **½ teaspoon pectin enzyme, if using unfiltered juice**
> **½ teaspoon grape tannin, or a cup of black tea**
> **1 packet yeast: Premier Cuvée or Lalvin KIV-1116**
> **7 teaspoons corn sugar, if making a sparkling perry**

1. Pour the juices into the primary fermenter. Stir in the yeast nutrient, pectin enzyme, and tannin (or tea).
2. Add the yeast, snap on the fermenter lid, and attach the airlock.
3. Fermentation is usually complete in 7 to 10 days. You can bottle it as is, or if you want a sparkling perry, add 7 teaspoons of corn sugar and bottle the perry in Champagne-style bottles, beer bottles, or soda bottles. Whether you make a still or sparkling perry, you don't need to age it more than a couple of weeks, but it does become better conditioned after a couple of months.

Serving Suggestion: Served chilled in a white wine glass with blue or creamy cheeses.

Beers

I am a firm believer in the people. If given the truth they can be depended upon to meet any national crisis. The great point is to bring them the real facts . . . and beer.

—*Abraham Lincoln*

BEER IS NORMALLY defined as a low-alcohol beverage brewed with malt and flavored with hops. In this section we will use a broader definition of beer: a low-alcohol, carbonated beverage, with malt and hops optional.

Unlike the beer you can make at home, almost all commercially produced brews today are dead, dead, dead. Before it's bottled, canned, or kegged, commercial beer is pasteurized to help keep it from going stale. After all, it may be in those containers for months before you drink it. Pasteurization not only kills the yeast and microbes, it also makes the beer's taste deteriorate more quickly. To carbonate it, beer manufacturers pressurize beer with carbon dioxide.

But for nearly all of the six thousand years of documented booze-swilling history, beer was served fresh and alive. The brewing of beer probably predates written history; it may even predate the invention of bread.

Here are a few historical footnotes regarding beer:

- The Code of Hammurabi, the world's oldest legal document, includes laws governing the brewing, distribution, and purchasing of beer. The penalty for violating some of these laws was death. Obviously there were some serious beer drinkers back then.
- By 4000 BC, a Babylonian consumer could buy sixteen kinds of beer in his local brewpub.
- Rice beer was a common drink in China by about 2300 BC.
- An Assyrian tablet from around 2000 BC claims that Noah, like many modern boaters, packed beer on his ark.
- Around 1100 BC, Egyptian king Ramses III sacrificed thirty thousand gallons of beer to the gods annually. His priests poured it on the altar, though a bit of it must have found its way through the holy men.
- The Aztecs had a myriad of gods associated with brewing pulque (agave beer).
- When Columbus arrived in the New World, he saw women making corn beer. Also, some of the first European settlers were offered persimmon beer by the local natives.
- The Puritans' consumption of beer was restricted by law; an individual was allowed no more than ½ gallon for breakfast. How far removed we are from our pious forefathers . . .
- William Penn, Thomas Jefferson, Samuel Adams, and George Washington were all brewers.

Historically and commercially, most beer was and is produced using the all-grain method: Barley is sprouted and toasted to make malt, which is then dried, ground, and simmered in water to extract the sugar. The resulting liquid wort is then mixed with other flavorings, such as hops, and fermented. While all-grain brewing is not particularly difficult to do, especially for people used to cooking, making great beverages easily is one of the themes of this book, so we will limit our recipes to an alternative method of brewing: using malt extracts. Many of those extracts include hops flavoring.

Hops are the preferred bittering and antimicrobial agent for beers and have been for the last few hundred years. Without something to counteract the sweetness of barley malt, the resulting brew is bland. Also, since the alcohol level of beer is low, the beverage is more open to contamination by bacteria if an antimicrobial substance, such as hops, isn't added. But using hops to bitter and preserve the beer was not always the preferred choice. Hops are bitter, aromatic, and cheap to grow; they help kill microbes and contain tannins that help to preserve beer; but they are also soporific, meaning they make imbibers sleepy, and they are estrogenic, meaning they can retard erections in male drinkers. The term "brewer's droop" refers to the disappointing experience of brewers who handle a lot of hops. Beer drinkers who favor strongly hopped beers can have a similar experience.

The use of hops instead of other bittering herbs, called gruits, was an economic decision and perhaps a religious one, since some of the gruit ales were reputed to have aphrodisiac qualities. Beers made with gruit were also brewed to have psychoactive qualities. Pilsner, for example, was originally bittered with henbane rather than hops. Henbane is a member of the nightshade family and has a long history of making its users seriously berserk.

So rather than always drinking hopped beer, you might want to try recipes that use alternative bittering agents with different effects than hops.

Beer Kits

We homebrewers can now purchase a wide variety of malt extracts, made from malted grains, to brew beer. The water is extracted, and the resulting syrup or powder is canned or bagged.

These extracts can be purchased either with or without hops and in all varieties and styles of beer, from a light pilsner or the popular U.S. lager to German bock, English stout, Scottish red ale, Australian ale, or wheat beer. And although using the extract method is more expensive than all-grain brewing, it's still a fraction of what you would spend in a store for beer of similar—or lesser—quality. It's also ridiculously easy, and the beer is so good that once you've made a few batches, you'll wonder why you didn't do it sooner.

Making beer from extract can be as simple as pouring a can of malt syrup into your sanitized primary fermenter, adding the proper amount of boiling water, letting the liquid cool, tossing in the yeast, snapping on the fermenter lid, and attaching an airlock. Within a week the beer is ready to bottle, and a couple of weeks later it's ready to drink.

To make a better beer, it's a good idea to cool the wort quickly. All-grain brewers employ a radiator-like device called a wort chiller to do this, but brewers using malt syrups have a simpler way to chill the wort. Since a can of malt syrup (and a couple of pounds of sugar) will make 6 gallons of brew, boil the syrup and sugar in 2 gallons of water, pour it in the primary fermenter, and chill it by adding cold water until the total amount reaches 6 gallons. Pouring in cold water has the additional benefit of pushing oxygen into the wort, and yeast needs some oxygen early in its growth cycle to reproduce.

Strong Waters

Notes:

- Choosing among various beer kits, especially if you shop the Internet, can be difficult. A good approach is to determine the variety of beer you want to make, then use an Internet search engine to look for it. Read the descriptions, pick your manufacturer, then search for that manufacturer and kit name to find the best price. Once I find a brand I like, I usually buy half a dozen cans of their malt because it keeps well and I save on shipping.

- The amount of water you add when making a beer kit is different from the amount added for the recipes in this book. The directions in a beer kit will tell you to add water to the malt syrup until the total volume of syrup and water equals, for example, 6 gallons. You do not, to continue the example, add a full 6 gallons of water to a can of malt, since you would end up with more than 6 gallons of beer and the result would be a little watery.

  Most of the recipes in this book that involve water instruct you to add 1 gallon. So when you add the remaining ingredients—for example, sugar—you will produce slightly more than 1 gallon of beer. Standardizing the recipes to 1 gallon of added water makes it easier for you to measure and to calculate when making larger batches.

Basic Beer

IN THE EIGHTEENTH century, Robert Burns wrote his version of the timeless tale of John Barleycorn. The poem not only outlines the process for making beer, it also anthropomorphizes barley as a Christlike figure who, after being mercilessly abused and killed by his enemies, has a triumphant "spiritual" rebirth.

There was three kings into the east,
    Three kings both great and high,
And they have sworn a solemn oath
    John Barleycorn should die.

They took a plough and plough'd him down,
    Put clods upon his head,
And they have sworn a solemn oath
    John Barleycorn was dead.

But the cheerful Spring came kindly on,
    And show'rs began to fall;
John Barleycorn got up again,
    And sore surpris'd them all.

The sultry suns of Summer came,
  And he grew thick and strong,
His head well arm'd wi' pointed spears,
  That no one should him wrong.

The sober Autumn enter'd mild,
  When he grew wan and pale;
His bending joints and drooping head
  Show'd he began to fail.

His colour sicken'd more and more,
  He faded into age;
And then his enemies began
  To show their deadly rage.

They've taen a weapon, long and sharp,
  And cut him by the knee;
Then tied him fast upon a cart,
  Like a rogue for forgery.

They laid him down upon his back,
  And cudgeled him full sore;
They hung him up before the storm,
  And turn'd him o'er and o'er.

They filled up a darksome pit
  With water to the brim,
They heaved in John Barleycorn,
  There let him sink or swim.

They laid him out upon the floor,
  To work him farther woe,
And still, as signs of life appear'd,
  They toss'd him to and fro.

They wasted, o'er a scorching flame,
  The marrow of his bones;
But a Miller us'd him worst of all,
  For he crush'd him between two stones.

And they have taen his very heart's blood,
  And drank it round and round;
And still the more and more they drank,
  Their joy did more abound.

John Barleycorn was a hero bold,
  Of noble enterprise,
For if you do but taste his blood,
  'Twill make your courage rise.

'Twill make a man forget his woe;
  'Twill heighten all his joy:
'Twill make the widow's heart to sing,
  Tho' the tear were in her eye.

Then let us toast John Barleycorn,
  Each man a glass in hand;
And may his great posterity
  Ne'er fail in old Scotland!

Making beer these days can be a simple process: no plows, carts, cudgels, or sharp weapons required, with the exception of a can opener.

Note: This recipe yields 1 gallon; however, most cans of pre-hopped malt are designed to make 6 gallons. The cans also include detailed instructions.

1 gallon water

⅔ cup (8 ounces) hopped malt syrup

⅔ cup (5 ounces) sugar

1 packet yeast: ale

7 teaspoons corn sugar

1. Heat the water and stir in the malt syrup and sugar. Note that malt syrup is heavier than water and will tend to sink to the bottom and burn if you don't mix it in well. Simmer the liquid until the syrup and sugar are totally dissolved.

2. Pour the liquid into the primary fermenter and let it cool to room temperature. Add the yeast, snap on the fermenter lid, and attach the airlock.

3. After 1 week the beer will finish fermenting. Add 7 teaspoons of corn sugar and bottle in Champagne-style bottles, beer bottles, or soda bottles.

4. Allow a minimum of 2 weeks to age, enough time for the beer to be conditioned—in other words, for the corn sugar to carbonate the beer, the yeast to settle to the bottom of the bottles, and the flavors to get acquainted.

Gruit Ale

AS MENTIONED IN the introduction to this section, through most of our beer drinking history, the brew hasn't been bittered with hops, but with other herbs. Hops, while providing an antibacterial quality and an astringent counterpoint to the sweetness of malt in beer, is burdened by being both soporific, meaning it makes imbibers sleepy, and estrogenic, meaning it can make men less manly.

However, for many centuries Europeans used familiar herbs to flavor and preserve their beers—and, beyond that, to add tonic and psychoactive qualities to the alcohol in their brew. So why the move away from using these alternatives, known as gruits, toward hops? Two intertwined reasons: economics and religion. The Catholic Church had a monopoly on commercial gruit production during the Middle Ages and charged more than the free market would bear. When Protestant groups wanted to break this monopoly, reduce prices, and perhaps reduce the level of intoxication, hops proved an ideal replacement. Note that, excepting price reduction, this change offered little benefit to the consumer. Can you imagine a beer ad like this: Drink our beer! It's not only cheaper, it also makes you sleepy and impotent!

As often happened, and still happens, we traded quality of experience for cost, conformity, and expedience. However, if you are ready to try reversing that trend, here's a recipe for a brew that includes readily available herbs that provide a delicious alternative to hopped beer, as well as a different set of psychoactive qualities:

- **Yarrow** This widely available herb has been used to help heal internal and external infections as long as there have been people to use it; it was found in the grave of a Neanderthal man buried sixty thousand years ago and is mentioned in the literature of all herbalists. It was also widely used to increase the inebriating effects of beer.

- **Saint-John's-Wort** This benevolent plant's antidepressant, anti-inflammatory, antiviral, and antibacterial qualities are confirmed by its historic reputation and a wealth of empirical evidence.
- **Mugwort** One of the most sacred of European herbs, mugwort has antimicrobial and antibacterial effects. It's also traditionally been used to help regulate women's cycles and relieve nervous tension and depression.

Your initial reaction when first drinking the ale may be, "It's interesting," but try a couple of bottles. The overall aroma and flavor is wonderfully complex: a crisp, cidery nose with a pleasant astringency at the end.

1 tablespoon dried yarrow

1 heaping tablespoon dried Saint-John's-wort

1 tablespoon dried mugwort

1 gallon water

1¼ cups (1 pound) unhopped malt syrup

1 packet yeast: ale

7 teaspoons corn sugar

1. Put the herbs in a nylon straining bag and simmer them in 1 quart of the water for 30 minutes.
2. Remove the bag from the water, turn off the heat, and stir in the malt syrup.
3. When the syrup has dissolved, pour the liquid into the primary fermenter, add the remaining 3 quarts of water, and let the liquid cool to room temperature.
4. Add the yeast, snap on the fermenter lid, and attach the airlock.
5. After 6 or 7 days, the ale should finish fermenting. Add 7 teaspoons of corn sugar and bottle in Champagne-style bottles, beer bottles, or soda bottles.

6. Wait a minimum of 3 weeks to allow the corn sugar to carbonate the beer, the yeast to settle to the bottom of the bottles, and the flavors to mix.

Serving Suggestion: Serve ice cold in a pint glass; consume with a beer-loving friend who is open to new experiences or a cider-drinker who doesn't like beer.

Ginger Ale

ALTHOUGH WE NORMALLY think of ginger ale as a soft drink, it was originally an alcoholic beverage consumed as both a refreshment and tonic. Ginger is an extremely healthful herb. It causes the heart to beat more strongly and slowly and can help reduce migraines. It helps remove cholesterol, it has antiviral, anti-inflammatory, and antibiotic properties, and it helps alleviate nausea. It may also be an aphrodisiac for both men and women.

This recipe makes a refreshing and complex ale: smooth malt up front, followed by a crisp blast of ginger and a spicy pepper finish. If you want a bolder ale, leave the bag of ginger and jalapeño in the fermenter until you bottle.

> **3 ounces ginger, peeled and sliced**
> **½ jalapeño, sliced (optional)**
> **1 gallon water**
> **1¼ cups (1 pound) unhopped malt syrup**
> **Juice of 1 lemon**
> **1 packet yeast: ale**
> **7 teaspoons corn sugar**

1. Put the ginger and jalapeño in a nylon straining bag and simmer them in 1 quart of the water for 30 minutes.
2. Remove the bag from the water, turn off the heat, and stir in the malt syrup.
3. When the syrup has dissolved, add the lemon juice.
4. Pour the hot liquid into the primary fermenter, add the remaining 3 quarts of water, and let it cool to room temperature. Add the yeast, snap on the fermenter lid, and attach the airlock.
5. After 1 week the beer will finish fermenting. Add 7 teaspoons of corn sugar and bottle in Champagne-style bottles, beer bottles, or soda bottles.

6. Wait a minimum of 2 weeks to allow the corn sugar to carbonate the beer, the yeast to settle to the bottom, and the flavors to mix.

Serving Suggestion: Ginger ale, served cold in a pint glass, makes a refreshing summer drink and pairs well with Asian food.

Spruce Beer

THIS BEER HAS a wonderful aroma and a mild flavor that is reminiscent of cola. It was very popular in the northeast United States, Canada, and Scandinavian countries in the eighteenth century. It may take you an iced bottle or three to fully appreciate the taste. You can buy spruce essence at homebrewing stores. Since there are no hops to give it any bitterness, add acid blend during brewing to give it more zing. You can also add freshly squeezed lime or lemon just before drinking. Even without the additional citrus, there is a lot of vitamin C in this beer. Behold the power of pine!

To be more traditional, a colonial version can be made with molasses instead of malt. Be aware, though, that molasses-based beers are an acquired taste . . . and a taste that no one I know has acquired. But perhaps a touch of molasses would be a good addition.

> **1 gallon water**
> **1¼ cups (1 pound) unhopped light malt syrup**
> **1 teaspoon acid blend**
> **1 teaspoon spruce essence**
> **1 packet yeast: ale**
> **7 teaspoons corn sugar**

1. Heat the water and stir in the malt syrup and acid blend. Note that malt syrup is heavier than water and will tend to sink to the bottom and burn if you don't mix it in well. Simmer the liquid until the syrup is totally dissolved.
2. Pour the liquid into the primary fermenter, stir in the spruce essence, and let it cool to room temperature. Add the yeast, snap on the fermenter lid, and attach the airlock.
3. After 1 week the beer should finish fermenting. Add 7 teaspoons of corn sugar and bottle in Champagne-style bottles, beer bottles, or soda bottles.

4. Wait at least 2 weeks before drinking this beer. It ages well, so save a few bottles to drink in 5 or 6 months.

Serving Suggestion: Serve cold in a pint glass.

Sumac Ale

THE RED BERRIES of the sumac tree have been used by every people who have lived in its vicinity to make lemony drinks, medicines, and wines and to spice their food. Since the name for the herb is similar in many Eurasian languages—English, French, Spanish, German, Italian, and also Arabic, Farsi, and Hebrew—its use probably predates any of the languages that share the word.

Herbal texts prescribe the berries and their powder as a digestive and a fever-reducer. Native Americans made a beverage similar to a beer using the sumac found in North America. This recipe makes a light red ale that has a refreshing citrus accent, and because the berries have a lot of tannin, it ages well. You can find sumac powder in most Middle Eastern grocery stores.

> ¼ **cup sumac powder**
> 1 **gallon water**
> 1¼ **cups (1 pound) unhopped light malt syrup**
> 1 **packet yeast: ale**
> 7 **teaspoons corn sugar**

1. Put the sumac powder in a muslin bag, not a nylon straining bag. Muslin has a tighter weave than the nylon used for straining bags and will hold the spice better. You can get muslin bags at herb shops. Simmer the sumac in the water for 1 hour. Remove the bag.

2. Stir in the malt syrup. Note that malt syrup is heavier than water and will tend to sink to the bottom and burn if you don't mix it in well.

3. Pour the hot liquid into the primary fermenter and let it cool to room temperature. Add the yeast, snap on the fermenter lid, and attach the airlock.

4. After 1 week, the beer will finish fermenting. Add 7 teaspoons of corn sugar and bottle in Champagne-style bottles, beer bottles, or soda bottles.

5. Wait at least 3 weeks to allow the corn sugar to carbonate the beer, the yeast to sink to the bottom, and the sumac flavor to settle in.

Serving Suggestion: This drinks more like a cider than a beer. Serve chilled in a pint glass with mild cheeses.

Persimmon Beer

VARIETIES OF PERSIMMON are native to both China and the United States. Algonquians introduced colonists to a beerlike beverage made from the fruit, and the thirsty and resourceful settlers modified the recipe to make a more familiar beverage.

Persimmon beer continued to be made wherever the trees grew; the recipe evolved, particularly in the South, until the early twentieth century. Traditional Southern recipes frequently describe mashing the fruit with cornmeal, baking it into cakes, and then pouring water on the cakes and fermenting the liquid.

With modern ingredients available, here is a simpler and tastier recipe. Fresh persimmons are only available in late fall and can be expensive. The dried fruit is available in Asian grocery stores, particularly in early February, around the Chinese New Year.

> 1 gallon water
> 1¼ cups (1 pound) unhopped light malt syrup
> 1 teaspoon acid blend
> 2 pounds dried persimmons, chopped, or 3 pounds fresh
>   persimmons, chopped
> Juice of 3 limes
> 1 packet yeast: Pasteur Champagne
> 7 teaspoons corn sugar

1. Heat the water and stir in the malt syrup and acid blend. Note that malt syrup is heavier than water and will tend to sink to the bottom and burn if you don't mix it in well. Simmer the liquid until the syrup and sugar are totally dissolved.

2. Put the persimmons in a nylon straining bag, add to the malt mixture, and simmer for 10 minutes.

3. Pour the liquid, including the bag of fruit, into the primary fermenter and let it cool to room temperature. Stir in the lime juice, then add the yeast. Snap on the fermenter lid and attach the airlock.

4. For the next few days, slosh the fermenter around or use a sanitized spoon to flip and moisten the bag of fruit.

5. After 1 week, remove the fruit bag, squeezing it gently to extract as much liquid as possible without pressing out any of the solids. Transfer the liquid to a secondary fermenter.

6. Since this beer includes dried fruit, it will take longer to finish. Wait 3 weeks, until all fermentation has stopped and any bits of fruit sink to the bottom.

7. Add 7 teaspoons of corn sugar and bottle in Champagne-style bottles, beer bottles, or soda bottles.

8. Wait a minimum of 1 month to allow enough time for the corn sugar to carbonate the beer, the yeast to settle to the bottom of the bottles, and the flavors to get acquainted.

Serving Suggestion: This beer has a mild apricot flavor and is best served very cold with grilled fish or by itself.

Apple Beer

BEER AND CIDER drinkers have many tastes in common, and appreciating this beverage is one of them. The flavor is popular enough that a mixed drink arose to take the place of the original beverage: the snakebite is a combination of half cider and half lager.

The original is even better than the bar re-creation. And while this simple recipe is a great place to start, feel free to adjust the ratio of apple to malt to better suit your tastes.

> 2½ **quarts water**
>
> 12 **ounces (1 scant cup) unhopped light malt syrup**
>
> 1 **quart pasteurized apple cider**
>
> ½ **teaspoon pectin enzyme, if using unfiltered cider**
>
> 1 **packet yeast: Pasteur Champagne**
>
> 7 **teaspoons corn sugar**

1. Heat the water and stir in the malt syrup. Note that malt syrup is heavier than water and will tend to sink to the bottom and burn if you don't mix it in well. Simmer for 10 minutes.
2. Pour the hot liquid into the primary fermenter and let it cool to room temperature. Stir in the apple cider and pectin enzyme, then add the yeast. Snap on the fermenter lid and attach the airlock.
3. Wait until fermentation has stopped, usually after 1 week.
4. Add 7 teaspoons of corn sugar and bottle in Champagne-style bottles, beer bottles, or soda bottles.
5. Wait 2 weeks for the corn sugar to carbonate the beer, the yeast to settle to the bottom of the bottles, and the flavors to get acquainted.

Serving Suggestion: Serve cold in a pint glass, with barbecue or other spicy food.

Heather Ale

ROBERT LOUIS STEVENSON wrote *Heather Ale: A Galloway Legend*, in which the last two surviving Pict men, the short native inhabitants of the country now known as Scotland, tricked the ninth-century Scottish king and retained the secret of the heather ale, which they had brewed for thousands of years.

From the bonny bells of heather
    they brewed a drink long-syne,
Was sweeter far than honey,
    was stronger far than wine.
They brewed it and they drank it,
    and lay in a blessed swound
For days and days together
    in their dwellings underground.
There rose a king in Scotland,
    a fell man to his foes,
He smote the Picts in battle,
    he hunted them like roes.
Over miles of the red mountain
    he hunted as they fled,
And strewed the dwarfish bodies
    of the dying and the dead.
Summer came in the country,
    red was the heather bell;
But the manner of the brewing
    was none alive to tell.
In graves that were like children's
    on many a mountain head,
The Brewsters of the Heather
    lay numbered with the dead.
The king in the red moorland
    rode on a summer's day;

Strong Waters

And the bees hummed, and the curlews
    cried beside the way.
The king rode, and was angry,
    black was his brow and pale,
To rule in a land of heather
    and lack the Heather Ale.
It fortuned that his vassals,
    riding free on the heath,
Came on a stone that was fallen
    and vermin hid beneath.
Rudely plucked from their hiding,
    never a word they spoke:
A son and his aged father–
    last of the dwarfish folk.
The king sat high on his charger,
    he looked on the little men;
And the dwarfish and swarthy couple
    looked at the king again.
Down by the shore he had them;
    and there on the giddy brink—
"I will give you life, ye vermin,
    for the secret of the drink."
There stood the son and father
    and they looked high and low;
The heather was red around them,
    the sea rumbled below.
And up and spoke the father,
    shrill was his voice to hear:
"I have a word in private,
    a word for the royal ear.
Life is dear to the aged,
    and honour a little thing;

I would gladly sell the secret,"
    quoth the Pict to the King.
His voice was small as a sparrow's,
    and shrill and wonderful clear:
"I would gladly sell my secret,
    only my son I fear.
For life is a little matter,
    and death is nought to the young;
And I dare not sell my honour
    under the eye of my son.
Take *him*, O king, and bind him,
    and cast him far in the deep;
And it's I will tell the secret
    that I have sworn to keep."
They took the son and bound him,
    neck and heels in a thong,
And a lad took him and swung him,
    and flung him far and strong,
And the sea swallowed his body,
    like that of a child of ten;—
And there on the cliff stood the father,
    last of the dwarfish men.
"True was the word I told you;
    only my son I feared;
For I doubt the sapling courage
    that goes without the beard.
But now in vain is the torture,
    fire shall never avail:
Here dies in my bosom
    the secret of Heather Ale."

Strong Waters

There is a suggestion that the secret of the Pict's brew was the timing of the heather harvest. Under some conditions, heather develops a blush, a white growth that not only adds a distinctive flavor, but may provide additional psychoactive qualities. The recipe may also have included bog myrtle, or sweet gale, which was also used in beer, both as a bittering agent and for its recreational psychoactive qualities.

While the Pict's legendary recipe may have died out, other, less reticent northern European Celtic people also made ale with the herb.

3 cups fresh heather tops, or 2 cups dried heather tops
1 gallon water
1¼ cups (1 pound) hopped malt extract
1 packet yeast: ale
7 teaspoons corn sugar

1. Put the heather in a nylon straining bag and simmer in the water for 30 minutes.
2. Remove the bag, squeezing it gently to extract as much liquid as possible without pressing out any of the solids. Turn off the heat and stir in the malt syrup. Note that malt syrup is heavier than water and will tend to sink to the bottom and burn if you don't mix it in well.
3. Pour the hot liquid into the primary fermenter and let it cool to room temperature. Add the yeast, snap on the fermenter lid, and attach the airlock.
4. After 1 week the beer will finish fermenting. Add 7 teaspoons of corn sugar and bottle in Champagne-style bottles, beer bottles, or soda bottles.
5. This beer changes over time. Try a bottle after a couple of weeks and then again in 2 or 3 months.

Serving Suggestion: Serve lightly chilled in a pint glass. Since the beer includes hops, you could serve this with any pub-style food.

Beerlike Quaffs

EVEN CONSIDERING THE loose definition of beer used in this book, there are beverages that drink like beer but don't contain hops or malt. The recipes in this section, more than any others in the book, reflect the types of beverages only available to the people who make them. Until very recently, none of these beverages were available commercially; they were simple to make, quick to finish, tasty, and inexpensive.

Pulque

PULQUE IS MADE by fermenting the juice of the agave, the same plant that yields tequila and mescal. No one knows for sure which group of pre-Hispanic Americans first made pulque, but the drink was sacred to all of them. The Aztecs of what is now Mexico worshipped many gods, and one group of them, the Centzon Totochtin, were an enormous drove of four hundred sacred and drunken rabbits, each representing a different type of intoxication. It's traditional when drinking pulque to slosh a little on the floor as a sacrifice to Ometochtli, or Two Rabbit.

> **3 quarts water**
> **1 quart agave nectar**
> **1 teaspoon acid blend**
> **1 teaspoon yeast nutrient**
> **1 packet yeast: Pasteur Champagne**
> **7 teaspoons corn sugar**

1. Heat the water and stir in the agave nectar, acid blend, and yeast nutrient. Note that agave nectar is heavier than water and will tend to sink to the bottom and burn if you don't mix it in well. Simmer until the agave nectar is totally dissolved.

2. Pour the hot liquid into the primary fermenter and let it cool to room temperature. Add the yeast, snap on the fermenter lid, and attach the airlock.

3. After 1 week the pulque should finish fermenting. It's traditionally cloudy, so feel free to bottle it before it clears. Add 7 teaspoons of corn sugar and bottle in Champagne-style bottles, beer bottles, or soda bottles.

4. Wait two weeks before drinking this beverage. Note that pulque will eventually clear, so if you don't drink it within a couple

of months, the cloudiness will settle to the bottom of the bottles. Not a problem—just pour carefully if you want a clear beverage.

Serving Suggestion: Pulque is a surprising and pleasant prelude to a Cinco de Mayo dinner or any Mexican meal; serve cold in a pint glass.

> **Kvass is the common beverage of all of Siberia. No matter what part of the country the traveler is in, and what kind of people he may be with at the time, he is more or less certain of being requested to partake of kvass.**
> —*Edward R. Emerson*, **Beverages Past and Present**

KVASS IS A low-alcohol drink ubiquitous from Western Russia and Eastern Europe to Siberia and Mongolia. In many recipes kvass uses rye as the primary source of sugar, usually as bread and sometimes as flour. It also frequently includes berries or apples, herbs (particularly mint), and occasionally barley, wheat, or oats, either as bread, meal, or flour. In some areas the solids were strained out; in others, the whole mass was consumed—a sort of a boozy Russian smoothie.

This recipe uses extra sugar to increase the alcohol level and corn sugar to carbonate it. Traditionally kvass was drunk as soon as the bread was removed, but for this recipe you should age the beverage for at least a month. There are two reasons for this: Like other sparkling beverages, it takes a couple of weeks to carbonate properly. And kvass initially has a slight salt flavor from the bread that seems to dissipate during aging. If you want a more traditional version, leave out the sugars, but be sure to either store it in the refrigerator or drink it soon after making.

> 1½ **gallons water**
> 2½ **cups (1¼ pounds) sugar**
> 20 **herbal mint tea bags**
> 1 **pound dark rye bread, chopped**
> 1 **packet yeast: ale**
> 7 **teaspoons corn sugar**

1. Boil the water, then turn off the heat and stir in the sugar. When the sugar has dissolved, add the tea bags and steep for about 10 minutes. Cover the pot to hold the aromatics in.
2. Put the bread in a nylon straining bag, place the bag in the primary fermenter, and pour the tea over it.
3. When the liquid has cooled to room temperature, add the yeast. Snap on the fermenter lid and attach the airlock.
4. After 4 days, remove the bag of bread and press out the liquid. Even with a good squeeze, a third of the liquid will remain in the bread. Allow your children to fight over the moist, intoxicating glop before sending them off to the fields to harvest cabbage.
5. After another week, the kvass will finish fermenting. Add 7 teaspoons of corn sugar and bottle in Champagne-style bottles, beer bottles, or soda bottles. Age for at least 1 month, but note that, because of the protein in the rye, this beverage will never clear, so don't bother waiting for that.

Serving Suggestion: Serve kvass chilled in a pint glass as you would a fall or wintertime beer. Honor its heritage by sipping it next to a fire while reading Dostoyevsky.

Sima

VAPPU, THE MAY DAY holiday in Finland, marks the beginning of spring. To accompany the festivities, Finns traditionally consume a mildly alcoholic citrus drink called sima.

> **1 gallon water**
> **2 lemons**
> **1 cup (8 ounces) granulated sugar**
> **1 cup (7 ounces) brown sugar**
> **1 packet yeast: ale**
> **7 teaspoons corn sugar**
> **¼ cup raisins**

1. Peel the lemons and scrape the white pith from the peels so that only the zest remains. Coarsely chop the zest and put it in the primary fermenter.
2. Juice the now-skinless lemons.
3. Boil the water, then stir in the sugars. Pour the hot liquid onto the lemon zest in the fermenter.
4. When the liquid has cooled to room temperature, stir in the lemon juice and add the yeast. Snap on the fermenter lid and attach the airlock.
5. In 4 or 5 days, the beverage should finish fermenting. Add 7 teaspoons of corn sugar and bottle in Champagne-style bottles, beer bottles, or soda bottles. Put a few raisins in each bottle.
6. This beverage isn't meant to age. Traditionally, when the raisins are plump, it's ready to drink.

Serving Suggestion: This sweet drink is best served chilled in a juice glass for an after-meal toast.

Kykeon

Metaneira filled a cup with sweet wine and offered it to Demeter; but she refused it, for she said it was not lawful for her to drink red wine, but bade them mix meal and water with soft mint and give her to drink. And Metaneira mixed the draught and gave it to the goddess as she bade. So the great queen Deo received it to observe the sacrament.

—*Homer, "Hymn to Demeter"*

KYKEON WAS AN ancient beerlike drink, humble yet sacramental. For about two thousand years, many Greeks—men, women, and slaves—took part in a ritual now known as the Mysteries. And even though a hundred generations of literate people took part in the event, they knew how to keep a secret, so there's still a lot we don't know about the Mysteries.

We do know that the Mysteries, which celebrate spring and agriculture, were taught to mankind by the goddess Demeter, who was called Ceres by the Romans. Ceres is where our word *cereal* comes from, and the barley-based peasant drink that the goddess quaffs was used by the Mystery initiates to break their ritual fast.

There's some supposition that the barley used in the initiates' drink contained opium or was infected with the ergot fungus, either of which would provide psychoactive properties. Aside from the ritual version of the drink, a less stimulating version of kykeon was also consumed by peasants for refreshment and sustenance.

The Iliad and *The Odyssey* both describe kykeon's ingredients as including barley, water, honey, pennyroyal, thyme, other herbs, goat cheese, and magic. Since some of the ingredients are illegal, poisonous, and, in the case of magic, hard to find when you really need it, I'm not including a recipe. If you come up with a version of kykeon that doesn't make you insane or get you arrested, send me the recipe for the next edition. Well, even if it doesn't work out, let me know what happens.

Infusions (and Distillations and Jackings)

ALCOHOL DISTILLATION IS the process of gently heating an alcoholic beverage to alcohol's boiling point of 179°F, cooling the resulting steam back into liquid, and capturing the resulting skullpop.

Distillation has been used by herbalists, physicians, and beverage makers to extract essential oils from herbs, nuts, and flowers and to extract alcohol from beer and wine for at least four thousand years. The practice really took off in the Middle Ages, when Europeans learned improved methods of distillation from the Arabs. Brandy was the first alcoholic distillate and was referred to as *aqua vitae*, the "water of life." It was originally considered to be

Strong Waters

extremely healthful by itself and even more so when infused with medicinal herbs.

Brandy was also occasionally used as a topical medicine, although the practice fell out of favor for a while during the fourteenth century. The physicians for France's Charles the Bad had him sewn in linen that was soaked in brandy in the hope that the treatment might change his poor health. The procedure was successful in a way; one of the female attendants who was sewing his cocoon closed used a candle flame to trim a thread, which set fire to the king and burned him to death.

This book does not advocate distillation. Not only does it require specialized equipment, but if you don't know what you're doing, a poisonous level of methanol may concentrate in your beverages, meaning if you drank enough of the stuff, you might end up selling pencils out of a tin cup on a street corner. Stills have also been known to catch fire or blow up. Finally, it's illegal to distill alcohol without a license.

Jacking, like distillation, is a method of separating alcohol from water to increase the strength of a beverage. Unlike distillation, jacking is done by freezing a fermented beverage until ice forms on the edges or the liquid becomes slushy. The unfrozen liquid is then poured off or put into cheesecloth and squeezed out. The unfrozen liquid is liquor with a higher percentage of alcohol.

This freezing process is used to produce eisbock lager (ice strong beer), which is made by freezing beer and then separating the ice from the remaining sweet and strong liquor. A similar process is used to create what are now called *ice beers*.

The potency of a jacked beverage depends on the temperature applied to the original beverage; the colder the liquor, the more water can be frozen out of it and the higher the percentage of alcohol in the remaining liquid. In New England, where this technique was historically used, people could get applejack to around 30 percent alcohol if winter temperatures went down to minus 20°F. Today, a freezer (set to 0°F) could be used to attain an alcohol concentration of almost 20 percent.

How Temperature Affects Alcohol Percentage

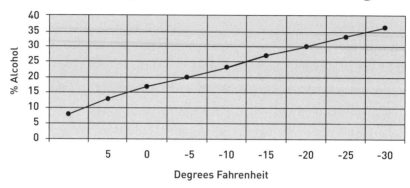

Jacking shares two characteristics with distillation:

- It's illegal. So, unless you want jackbooted AFT agents kicking down your door in the middle of the night, don't freeze fermented beverages to increase their alcohol level.
- Jacking concentrates both ethanol and poisonous methanol in the remaining beverage. The morning-after affects from regularly drinking too much applejack, made from frozen apple cider, were sometimes described as having "apple palsy."

Given the issues associated with distillation and jacking, the recipes in this section involve using commercially available distilled spirits to make infusions.

Infusions Using Distilled Spirits

Infusions are made by soaking herbs, spices, or fruit in a distilled spirit such as brandy or vodka to extract their essences. While alcohol was originally just a solvent used to capture concentrated botanicals, over time alcohol became the primary ingredient with the herbal or fruit aspects as flavorings. The recipes in this section reflect a range of infusions from medicinal to recreational.

Nocino

JUNE 21, THE LONGEST DAY of the year and the height of the growing season, has been celebrated in the northern hemisphere as the summer solstice, Midsummer Day, Balder's Day, and Saint John's Day. Included in the Italian version of the festivities was the making of a walnut aperitif called nocino.

Although the drink is started on the longest day of the year, it's often consumed on the shortest, the winter solstice, popularly known as Christmas. Not only is the drink a good digestive during a season of overeating, it's also a liquid reminder that summer will come again.

> **21 green walnuts, picked on June 21**
> **2 sticks cinnamon**
> **4 whole cloves**
> **5 roasted coffee beans**
> **Zest of 2 lemons**
> **About 1 quart brandy**
> **1 cup (8 ounces) sugar**

1. Rinse the walnuts and cut them lengthwise into quarters, husks and all. At this time of year, walnuts are more like a vegetable than a nut, so it isn't as hard as it sounds. Note that even though walnut juice at this stage looks clear, it will stain anything it touches as it dries, so roll up your sleeves and wash your hands immediately afterward.

2. Place the cinnamon, cloves, coffee beans, and zest in a 1 quart jar. Add enough walnuts to fill the remaining space. Top off with brandy and screw on the lid.

3. Put the jar a sunny place. After about 2 months, the liquid will turn dark. Strain out the solids. About 2 cups of liquid should remain.

4. Add the cup of sugar and enough brandy to refill the jar.

5. Let the nocino stand for at least another month. Sediment will drop to the bottom, so carefully pour the liquid into another container and age until Christmas.

Note: If your nocino isn't as dark as you would like, put 3 black tea bags into the liquid and leave them there for a few days. I won't tell anyone.

Serving Suggestion: Nocino is the ultimate digestive after a winter holiday meal. Serve at room temperature in a tiny glass.

Strong Waters

Rosolio

SO MANY MEMORABLE things came out of the Italian Renaissance: paintings by da Vinci, sculptures by Michelangelo, orgies by Pope Alexander VI, and this medicinal libation created by a Paduan doctor. The original recipe used brandy, but you may want to substitute vodka to savor more of the rose bouquet.

> **1 quart rose blossoms, loosely packed**
> **1 vanilla bean, or ¼ teaspoon vanilla extract**
> **1 cup (8 ounces) sugar**
> **About 1 quart vodka or brandy**

1. Gather the roses in the late morning or early afternoon, after the dew has lifted but before the day becomes hot.
2. Remove the petals from the sepal, the green section that connects the petals to the stem. Fill a 1-quart jar loosely with petals. Add the vanilla, sugar, and enough of the vodka to fill the jar. Screw on the lid and store in a dark place.
3. After 2 weeks, strain the beverage through cheesecloth to remove the petals and vanilla bean. Return the liquid to the jar, top off with vodka, and store in a dark place.
4. After an additional 2 weeks, check the jar to see if any particles have dropped to the bottom. If so, pour the clear liquid into a clean jar. You don't need to age this.

Serving Suggestion: Serve at room temperature in a small glass between dinner courses as a palate cleanser.

Limoncello

Victory has a hundred fathers, but defeat is an orphan.
—Galeazzo Ciano

LIMONCELLO IS PERHAPS Italy's greatest gastronomical gift to the twentieth century—at least the greatest one involving lemons. Like all mysterious and delicious Italian progeny, several fathers claim paternity: Sorrento, Capri, and Amalfi. While different lemon types yield different-tasting beverages, try to get organic or at least pesticide-free fruit. This recipe uses a lot of zest, and even washing lemons doesn't remove the pesticides that have soaked into the skin. Many people prefer Meyer lemons for their aroma and mild level of acid.

Zest of 6 lemons
1½ cups (12 ounces) sugar
About 1 quart vodka

1. Peel the lemons and scrape the white pith from the peels so that only the zest remains.
2. Put the zest in a 1-quart jar. Add the sugar and enough of the vodka to fill the container. Screw on the lid and store in a dark place.
3. After 2 months, strain the beverage through cheesecloth to remove the zest. Return the liquid to the jar and add enough vodka to top off the jar. You don't need to age this.

Serving Suggestion: Serve very cold in a small glass after an Italian dinner. If you've got at least four people at the table, be prepared to go through a bottle.

Violatium

THE ANCIENT ROMANS made this exotic and beautiful wine infusion. Keep in mind that while violets have prodigious amounts of vitamin C, they can also trigger a spectacular bout of diarrhea if you consume too many.

Note that a quart of violets may be hard to come by all at once. You can pick and freeze blossoms until you have enough, or make a proportionally smaller batch. It took a couple of seasons to collect enough for my first batch.

> **1 quart violet blossoms, loosely packed**
> **1 cup (³/₄ pound) honey: orange blossom or clover**
> **About 1 quart mild white wine, such as Chenin Blanc**

1. Strip the blossoms from the stems. The sepal, the green cap at the bottom of the blossom, can remain. Fill a 1-quart jar with blossoms. Add the honey and enough of the wine to fill the jar. Screw on the lid and store in a dark place.

2. After 2 months, strain the beverage through cheesecloth to remove the petals. Return the liquid to the jar and add enough wine to top off the jar.

3. After an additional 2 weeks, check the jar to see if any sediment has dropped to the bottom. If it has, pour the clear liquid into a clean jar. You don't need to age this.

Serving Suggestion: Serve at room temperature in a small glass between courses as a palate cleanser.

Anise Liqueur

EVERY COUNTRY THAT has anise seems to make an aperitif out of it: Greece has ouzo; Turkey their raki; Israel and the Arab and Persian countries all drink arak; Italy has anisette and Sambuca; France produces Pastis. While all these liquors are made though distillation, you can create a fair substitute with an infusion. More importantly, you might tailor this simple recipe over time to include other spices or herbs. See the recipe for absinthe (page 202) as an example.

3 tablespoons anise seed
2 cups (1 pound) sugar
About 1 quart vodka

1. Crush the seeds lightly and put them in a muslin bag, not a nylon straining bag. Muslin has a tighter weave than the nylon used for straining bags and will hold the spice better. You can get muslin bags at herb shops.
2. Put the bag and sugar in a 1-quart jar. Add enough of the vodka to fill the jar. Screw on the lid.
3. After 2 weeks, remove the bag of spice.
4. Let the liquid stand for another 2 weeks. Check the jar to see if any sediment has dropped to the bottom. If it has, pour the clear liquid into a clean jar.
5. Age this for at least 3 months before drinking.

Serving Suggestion: Serve cold in a small glass. Anise liqueurs go well with seafood appetizers, such as clams, octopus, calamari, and sardines.

Raspberry Liqueur

THIS SIMPLE AND gorgeous infusion captures my favorite summer fruit. It can also be made with any fruit, especially other berries. It's a great ingredient when mixing cocktails, but I prefer it at room temperature all by itself.

> **2 pounds raspberries (6 cups)**
> **About 1 quart vodka**
> **1½ cups (12 ounces) sugar**

1. Put the berries in a small nylon straining bag, then put the bag in a 1-quart jar and mash them gently in the jar. Add the sugar and enough of the vodka to fill the jar. Store in a dark place.
2. After two weeks, remove the bag, squeezing it gently to extract as much liquid as possible without pressing out any of the solids. Add enough vodka to fill the jar.
3. After an additional 2 weeks, the remaining fruit bits will have sunk to the bottom. Pour the clear liquid into a clean jar. You don't need to age this.

Serving Suggestion: Serve at room temperature in a small glass after dinner. It's also good with chocolate desserts.

Irish Cream Whiskey

COLONIALS IN NEW ENGLAND used to make a drink called a flip by filling a mug with whiskey or rum, eggs, sugar, and spices and then placing a hot poker into the mixture. The poker caramelized some of the sugars and put a warm foamy head on the drink. Commercial versions of the flip, such as the recipe below, were packaged in the 1970s—no fireside assembly required.

2 cups Irish whiskey

1 cup half-and-half

1 14-ounce can sweetened condensed milk

2 tablespoons sweetened chocolate syrup

1 teaspoon instant coffee

1 teaspoon vanilla extract

1 teaspoon almond extract

½ teaspoon coconut extract (optional)

Mix all of the ingredients in a blender, then refrigerate before serving. The beverage will keep in the refrigerator for a couple of months, or in the freezer indefinitely. Be sure to shake it before serving if it's been sitting for a while.

Serving Suggestion: Served chilled in a small glass after dinner.

Atholl Brose

A BROSE IS a Scottish dish of oatmeal and either water or milk. This lovely version is a drink attributed to an eighteenth-century Duke of Atholl, who purportedly filled his enemies' water well with this concoction during a Highland rebellion, which lead to his victory over them in battle. This tastes so good, maybe they lost interest in revolting.

> **1 cup old-fashioned rolled oats**
> **3 cups water**
> **¼ cup (3 ounces) honey**
> **1 cup whipping cream**
> **2 cups Scotch whisky**

1. Put the oats in a nylon straining bag and place the bag in a deep bowl. Add the water and let the oats steep overnight.
2. The next morning, squeeze the water out of the bag. Put the liquid in a saucepan, add the honey, and heat gently until the honey dissolves.
3. Stir in the cream, then add the whisky.
4. Refrigerate until cool before serving. The beverage will keep in the refrigerator for a couple of months, or in the freezer indefinitely.

Serving Suggestion: Serve chilled in a small glass after dinner. Also, I must confess, this has looked tempting in the refrigerator on Sunday mornings. It's got oatmeal in it, after all.

Absinthe

> After the first glass you see things as you wish they were. After the second, you see things as they are not. Finally you see things as they really are, and that is the most horrible thing in the world.
> —*Oscar Wilde*

AT THE BEGINNING of the twentieth century, absinthe was *the* romanticized drink of writers, painters, actors, and other scandalous ne'er-do-wells. As you might imagine, upstanding citizens were both intrigued and horrified. Newspapers contributed to both the drink's mystique and its decades-long ban.

The mystique peaked in 1905 when Jean Lanfray, a Swiss farmer and known absinthe abuser, shot his entire family. Newspaper stories highlighted his consumption of absinthe that day, although references to the numerous bottles of wine and other spirits also consumed before the slaughter were downplayed. This and other dark tales led good and fearful citizens to ban absinthe in most countries where it was made, with the exception of Spain and Czechoslovakia. In the late 1990s, the countries in the European Union lifted the ban, and in 2007 the United States did, as well.

The demonic ingredient in absinthe is the bitter herb wormwood, which, in addition to helping to expel worms from your digestive system, reputedly has psychoactive properties. Recent studies have cast doubts on the effects of wormwood, however. What may be more likely is that any heady effects of the beverage come from the synergy of the herbs used rather than just thujone, the active ingredient in wormwood.

Because the authentic beverage is distilled, the infusion recipe below will produce only an imitation.

Caution: Prolonged absinthe use can set off headaches, nervousness, and insomnia, and has caused already drunken Swiss farmers to shoot their families. This recipe is included for historic purposes only. Wormwood can be purchased at herb shops.

2 teaspoons anise seed
2 teaspoons angelica root
1 teaspoon dried wormwood
1 teaspoon marjoram
½ teaspoon coriander seed
½ teaspoon fennel seed
4 cardamom pods
2 cups (1 pound) sugar
About 1 quart vodka

1. Crush the spices lightly and put them in a muslin bag, not a nylon straining bag. Muslin has a tighter weave than the nylon used for straining bags and will hold the spices better. You can get muslin bags at herb shops.
2. Put the spices and sugar in a 1-quart jar and add enough of the vodka to fill the jar.
3. Remove the bag after 1 week.
4. Let the liquid stand for another 3 weeks. Check the jar to see if any sediment has dropped to the bottom. If it has, pour the clear liquid into a clean jar. Age this for at least 3 months before drinking.

Serving Suggestion: A dose of absinthe is traditionally served at room temperature in a wide glass. A specially designed slotted spoon is placed on top of the glass and a sugar cube placed on the spoon. Iced water is slowly dripped onto the cube, dissolving it and releasing the herbal oils in the liquor. It's also great to serve ice cold in an aperitif glass with seafood appetizers.

6

Troubleshooting

CHAPTER 2, the equipment chapter of this book, advises you to get a logbook and keep notes about your beverage making. If you're reading this section because something isn't right and you need to fix it, you'll be glad if you took notes, because the first step for these procedures is to review your notes.

> **Note:** If you end up with a batch of something that, while not terrible, isn't something you would take to someone's dinner party, don't pour it down the drain. If you have the space, bottle it and wait. Aging can contribute astonishing improvements to many rough beverages. And if aging doesn't improve it, consider serving it to those still-thirsty dinner guests who linger longer than politeness dictates is proper. They may still keep you awake longer than you want, but there is some satisfaction in watching them consume your failed experiments rather than the successful ones.

Following are some common problems, along with steps you can take to identify their causes and correct them.

My beverage isn't fermenting yet.

While most beverages start to ferment in 8 to 36 hours, sometimes fermentation can take longer to start. If your liquid hasn't started bubbling after 2 or 3 days, here is a list of considerations and actions you can take:

- *Was the liquid hot when you added the yeast?* If you heated the liquid to sanitize it—for example, when making beer—and then added the yeast when it was still hot, you may have killed much of the yeast. Add yeast only to a liquid that is at room temperature or cooler. Try adding another packet of yeast to your batch.
- *Is there oxygen in the liquid?* Yeast needs oxygen during its initial growth phase, so if you boiled the liquid or used distilled water, the yeast may not have enough oxygen to replicate properly. Try taking the airlock off and sloshing the primary fermenter around for a couple of minutes to splash some air into the liquid. Then add another packet of yeast and replace the airlock.
- *Did you wait long enough after adding a sulfite before adding the yeast?* If you used Campden tablets or some other form of sulfite to sanitize the liquid—for example, when making wine—you need to wait about 24 hours before adding the yeast. Also, compare your notes to the recipe and verify that you didn't add more sulfite than the recipe called for. If you think you added a lot more, wait an additional 24 hours before adding another packet of yeast.
- *Is the room temperature too high or low?* The yeasts in the recipes in this book work best when the temperature is between 68°F and 75°F. Try moving the liquid to a warmer or cooler location.
- *Is there too much sugar for the yeast to ferment?* You may find it tempting to add more sugar to a liquid than a recipe calls for to increase the alcohol level or sweetness of the finished beverage. However, if the sugar content is too high, the yeast may have trouble even starting. You can compare your notes to the recipe and verify that you used the correct amount of sugar, but the best way to check whether you have a viable amount of sugar is with a hydrometer. See the section on hydrometers (page 16) for details.

Generally a hydrometer level higher than 1.100 could inhibit wine yeasts, and a level higher than 1.040 makes ale yeasts choke. If there is too much sugar for the yeast you originally used, you can add a more alcohol-tolerant yeast such as Champagne yeast, or you could add water or juice to the fermentable liquid to dilute the sugar.

- *Is the pH too high or low?* Yeast works best, and bacteria growth is retarded, when the pH range is roughly between 3 and 4 for wine-like beverages and 5 and 6 for beerlike beverages. If you are making a beverage that includes an acidic fruit, such as cranberries or citrus fruit, it's possible that the liquid is too acidic for the yeast to ferment. You can check your recipe and verify that you used the correct amount of ingredients, but if you're not following a recipe, the simplest way to check a liquid's pH is with pH test strips. See the section on pH test strips (page 19) for details.

  Reduce acidity by adding small amounts of calcium carbonate to the liquid; increase acidity by adding acid blend. Take a 1 gallon sample of a beverage where the pH isn't in the right range, mix ¼ teaspoon of the calcium carbonate or acid blend with a little water, and stir it into the sample. When adding calcium carbonate, let it sit a few days to allow any residual to settle to the bottom. Compare the sample to the original. If the pH is in the correct range, make the same adjustment to the rest of the batch, add more yeast, and see if fermentation starts.

- *Does the liquid include enough nutrients?* While a lack of nutrients is seldom an issue with malt-based beverages such as beer, many beverages that contain fruit, flowers, or honey require more nutrients than the ingredients contain. Check the recipe and verify that you followed it. Try adding ½ teaspoon of yeast nutrient per gallon and another packet of yeast.

My beverage has stopped fermenting.

If the fermentation started but stopped after a day or two, here are a few considerations:

- *Maybe it's finished.* Beers and ciders sometimes finish fermenting in 1 or 2 days and wine can finish in 4 or 5 days if it's warm and there's not a lot of sugar for the yeast to ferment. A simple way to determine if the fermentation has finished is to add a couple of teaspoons of corn sugar to a beverage that is not currently bubbling the airlock. If you add the sugar and see surface foam, then your yeast is still viable and fermentation is complete. Once this last bit of sugar has been fermented, your beverage just needs to be stable and clear before bottling. However, the surest way to determine if your liquid has finished fermenting is to check the specific gravity with a hydrometer. See the section on hydrometers (page 16) for details. If the specific gravity is less than 1.000, the beverage is probably done fermenting.

- *Is the temperature too high?* Although some strains of yeast can initially ferment in temperatures of up to 90°F, toward the end of a fermentation a beverage's alcohol level is higher and the yeast is weaker from the toxicity. At this stage, keep the temperature between 70–80°F.

- *Was it ever bubbling?* Some liquids sputter for a few days and then stop. This is often an indication that the liquid doesn't have enough nutrients or acid to complete the fermentation. Compare your notes to the recipe and see if you followed it correctly. Add what seems to be lacking and another packet of yeast.

- *Was there too much sugar for the yeast to ferment?* Sometimes when there is too much sugar for the yeast to consume, the fermentation starts and then stops prematurely. Check your notes to verify that you followed the recipe. You can also use a hydrometer to check the amount of sugar in the liquid. Generally, a level higher than 1.100 can inhibit wine yeasts, and a level higher than 1.040 makes ale yeasts stall.

My beverage is cloudy (or hazy).

If you want your final beverage to be clear, here are a few considerations:

- *Has the liquid finished fermenting?* Even a liquid that is barely fermenting can be very cloudy. Watch the airlock carefully. If the airlock passes a bubble within 2 or 3 minutes, the liquid is still fermenting and you need to let it finish before determining whether it will clear naturally or not.
- *Have you waited long enough?* Most beverages will clear naturally if given enough time; this can range from a few days for beer and cider to several months for other beverages.
- *Are you fermenting a beverage that contains pectins?* Many types of fruit, such as apples, pears, citrus fruits, and elderberries, contain pectin, which can cause a beverage to be hazy, even after the fermentation has finished. Here are a few considerations for clearing pectin:
  - Pectin enzymes break this complex carbohydrate into smaller particles, which then react better to fining agents.
  - Bentonite is a fining agent that can also clear pectin haze.
  - Activated charcoal can clear a haze, though it will also remove some color and flavor.
- *Are you fermenting a beverage that contains proteins?* Many grain-based beverages will contain suspended particles of protein that can cause a beverage to be hazy. Here are a few considerations for clearing proteins:
  - Bentonite is a fining agent that can clear protein haze.
  - Egg whites are great at reducing protein haze. Because they don't affect color, they're especially useful with red wines.
  - Silica gel not only helps clear a protein haze, it also firms up sediment at the bottom of the fermentation vessel, which makes the liquid easier to siphon.
  - Isinglass helps remove protein, but it also removes yeast, so be sure that fermentation has finished before using this agent.

Strong Waters

- Activated charcoal can clear a haze, though it will also remove some color and flavor.
- *Irish moss* won't do anything to clear an existing protein haze, but make a note to use this next time you are cooking a similar batch to avoid this particular problem.
- *Sparkolloid* helps to clear protein haze and has little impact on flavor or color.

My beverage is fizzy when opened.

If the beverage is supposed to be still, or uncarbonated, but produces bubbles in the glass when poured, here are a few considerations:

- *Are there enough bubbles to make the beverage unpleasant to drink?* A slight amount of initial carbonation in the glass or a tingle on the tongue is a deliberate attribute known as *spritzig* in some styles of German wines and *frizzante* in Italian wines. Especially if the beverage is a light one, the bubbles may improve the experience.
- *Did you stabilize the beverage properly before bottling?* Although you don't need to use potassium metabisulfite or Campden tablets to stabilize a beverage, it's hard to be sure that the yeast is inactive if you don't. Also, even if the yeast is inactive, without sufficient stabilizers, alcohol-tolerant bacteria can cause what's known as *malolactic fermentation*, or MLF. The bacteria will convert the beverage's sharper-flavored malic acid into the softer and more buttery-flavored lactic acid. While some beverages benefit from the conversion, if it takes place after you bottle some carbonation will occur in the beverage.

  Check your notes and see if you added the equivalent of one crushed Campden tablet per gallon of beverage. If you haven't added enough stabilizer, you may want to rebottle the batch with the correct amount. Alternatively, you could store the bottles in a cool place so the corks don't pop and then decant the beverage before serving.

- *Did you remove the carbonation before the beverage was bottled?* Although we aren't normally aware of it, liquids contain small amounts of gas. If you've ever noticed the tiny bubbles in ice cubes, you've seen how water will freeze and leave the suspended air in the ice as pockets. Similarly, as yeast ferments, it puts carbon dioxide into the liquid. While most of this gas bubbles out of the airlock, some remains in the liquid, though you may not notice it until after you open a bottle. If you've checked your notes and determined that you used sufficient stabilizers, just be aware that this is an issue with this particular batch and decant the beverage before serving. For future batches, you may want to degas your beverage before bottling. See the section on degassers (page 20) for details.

My beverage smells bad.

Here are several reasons this can happen and some workarounds to help fix the issue.

- *Did you use too much sulfite when stabilizing the wine?* When multiplying ingredients to make a batch larger than the recipe you're working from, it's easy to miscalculate the amount of sulfite to use and put too much in. Compare your notes to the recipe. If you think you added too much sulfite, let the beverage sit for several months, then try tasting it again. The sulfite may have dissipated.
- *Were there sufficient nutrients or acid in the fermenting liquid?* If the smell resembles rotten eggs, it's possible that the amount of nutrients was insufficient for the yeast during fermentation. When this happens, the live yeast feed on dead ones, which causes an off flavor. Add 1 teaspoon of activated charcoal per gallon of beverage and let it sit for a couple of weeks. Charcoal sinks to the bottom, so it's relatively easy to pour off a glass and test whether the taste has improved. Winemakers used to drop copper pennies into their beverage to help remove this off taste, but I'm not sure how much copper there is in pennies anymore.

- *Does the beverage taste like cork?* Natural corks can be finicky things. If they come into contact with chlorinated water, they can interact with naturally occurring mold to create an off taste. Also, they don't always set or seal well. Look at the necks of other bottles in this batch and see if they are seated evenly. If any beverage has leaked past a cork and left some residue on the bottle neck, it could also indicate a problem with other corks in this batch. There isn't a fix for moldy or leaky corks. Set other bottles in this batch aside and remember to taste them carefully before serving.
- *Were the ingredients and the equipment sanitized?* Yeast has its share of competitors, which sometimes coexist in a beverage. The very few times I've had a contaminated batch, it wasn't a total surprise. I knew I wasn't as careful as I should have been. Pour the bottles back into a carboy and gently mix in one crushed Campden table per gallon to sanitize the beverage. Let the beverage sit in the carboy for a few weeks so the sulfite can dissipate. See if the flavor has improved.

Glossary

MANY OF THE TERMS in this glossary have already been explained where they occur in the text. However, because you may read other books, magazine articles, and Web pages, I also include them here for easy reference—along with some additional winemaking and brewing terms not used in this book.

ACID BLEND: Typically, a powdered blend of citric, tartaric, and malic acids. There are three reasons to add acid to a liquid you will ferment:

- Yeast works better in a slightly acidic environment.
- Many types of bacteria don't survive well in an acid solution.
- The taste of some beverages improves if acid is added.

ACIDULATION: A fancy term for adding acid to a fermenting liquid.

AIRLOCK: Also called a fermentation lock, or bubbler. A device that enables carbon dioxide to escape a fermentation container and prevents oxygen from entering.

AMELIORATION: Adding sugar or water.

AMYLASE ENZYME: Helps convert starches into fermentable sugars. Beer brewers sometimes use ¼ teaspoon per gallon to reactivate a stuck fermentation.

AROMA: The portion of a beverage's scent that originates from the ingredients.

ASTRINGENCY: The effect that tannin has on the mouth; it causes you to pucker and leaves a "dry" feeling.

ATTENUATION: The portion of sugars that a yeast will convert to alcohol. Different yeasts will convert different percentages of sugars to alcohol, enabling you to select a variety that will influence the amount of residual sugar.

AUTOLYSIS: When yeast cannibalizes other yeasts in the batch. It may be brought on by high temperatures or insufficient nutrition or acid for the yeast.

BEER: A fermented beverage containing water, malt, hops, and yeast. In most countries, many other ingredients may be added.

BENTONITE: A type of finely ground clay that is used as a clarifying agent. At any stage of fermentation, including the beginning, ½ teaspoon can be added to provide something that yeast can attach themselves to; this improves growth and helps clear out solids from the primary fermentation.

BODY: When tasting a beverage, this is the mouthfeel. You can also swirl a glass of a beverage and get some idea of the body from the film it leaves on the side of the glass. Wines are often described as either light-, medium-, or full-bodied.

BOUQUET: The part of a beverage's scent that develops as a result of aging.

BRAGGOT: A fermented beverage made with malt and honey; it's a cross between a mead and an ale.

CALCIUM CARBONATE: Used to lower the acidity of a beverage by raising the pH. Pure water has a pH of 7.0; liquids below 7.0 are acidic; those above 7.0 are alkaline. Yeast works best and bacteria growth is retarded when the range is roughly between 3.0 and 4.0 for winelike beverages and 5.0 to 6.0 for beerlike beverages. If the pH is below 3.0, fermentation may not be able to start. The amount you use varies. You can use pH strips to test whether your beverage falls within the right pH range,

CAMPDEN TABLETS: Tablets of a standard amount of compressed potassium or sodium metabisulfite, about the size of an aspirin; when crushed, each tablet will sanitize a gallon of liquid.

CAP: A winemaking term for the layer of fruit goo that forms on the top of the wine during the first phase of fermentation. Although the liquid will ferment under a solid cap, most winemakers break it up every day. This helps to keep the cap material moist and therefore deepens the color and flavor of the finished beverage. It also helps to prevent bacterial contamination.

CARBONIC MACERATION: This type of fermentation is used to create dark, fruity wines such as Beaujolais Nouveau. The process is as follows: Whole fruit is poured into a tall fermentation vessel that's sealed completely. The weight of the fruit on the top crushes the fruit on the bottom. As the broken fruit ferments, it releases carbon dioxide, which blankets the rest of the fruit. Therefore, the remaining fermentation takes place inside the berries in a process called intracellular fermentation. After a few days the fruit is removed, pressed, and fermented. Wines created with carbonic maceration feature low levels of tannin and are not as complex or likely to age well. However, since these beverages require little aging, they can be enjoyed soon after fermentation finishes.

CARBOY: Also known as a demijohn, this glass or plastic container resembles a watercooler bottle. They range in size from 3 to 15 gallons, but the most common size for home use is 6 gallons.

CIDER: Fermented juice, usually apple. In the United States, cider is usually called hard cider and has less than 8 percent alcohol.

CITRIC ACID: Used to increase acidity; as you might imagine, it adds a slight citrus taste.

CLEARING: The process of getting a beverage transparent by filtering, adding a fining agent, or letting time pass.

CONGENER: Impurities produced by yeast during fermentation; these by-products provide much of the taste, aroma, and color of the beverage. They may also contribute to hangovers.

Strong Waters

CORN SUGAR: Also known as dextrose, this sugar is primarily used for carbonating fermented beverages. Corn sugar, although slightly less sweet than regular table sugar made from sugar cane or beets, is almost completely consumed by yeast. Therefore, when used to make sparkling beverages, there is less residue in the bottle.

CUTE: From Rome's Golden Age through the Middle Ages, this "wine kit" was made from grape juice boiled down to a third of its original volume. In the Bible, the Babylonian king gives the Jews "wine" for their sacrifices as they leave captivity—but the literal translation is "a thick sticky syrup" so this "wine" could have actually been cute.

CUVÉE: The French term for a batch of wine.

CYSER: Cider with added honey, which produces a higher alcohol content. Another way to define a cyser is as an apple melomel.

DIAMMONIUM PHOSPHATE: Also known as DAP, this cheap, inorganic chemical is widely used in the wine industry as a yeast nutrient. Used incorrectly it can create off flavors or even stop a fermentation. It's better to use a yeast nutrient made from yeast hulls.

DISTILLATION: Distillation is the process of gently heating an alcoholic beverage to the alcohol's boiling point of 179°F, cooling the resulting steam back into liquid, and capturing it.

ESTERS: Certain fruity, floral, and spicy aromas that are retained or enhanced during fermentation and aging.

FERMENTATION: In the making of alcoholic beverages, this describes the anaerobic (without oxygen) consumption of sugars and nutrients by yeast to produce alcohol and carbon dioxide.

FERMENTER: Also called a fermentation container, this is where fermentation takes place. Fermentations that take over two weeks to complete are often done in two types of containers: starting in a primary fermenter, often made of food grade plastic, and finishing in a secondary fermenter, often a glass container called a carboy. Fermentations that complete in less than a couple of weeks are often done in just a primary fermenter.

Glossary

FINING: Fining is the use of a liquid or powder that absorbs or otherwise attaches itself to fine particles in the beverage and then drops to the bottom, so that clear liquid can be siphoned off.

FLOCCULATE: The clumping together of the yeast bits when they sink. A yeast type flocculates well when it forms a solid mass on the bottom of the fermentation container. This is an attribute to seek in a yeast, because it's easier to rack the clear liquid from the gunk if the whole mess stays put at the bottom of the fermenter.

GELATIN: A fining agent that removes tannins. Mix ½ teaspoon in warm water and blend it into 1 gallon of beverage.

FORTIFY: To fortify a beverage means to add a distilled spirit, such as bandy or vodka, to a fermented beverage to increase the level of alcohol. Port is the most commonly known fortified beverage and is made by adding grape brandy to partially fermented wine. The higher level of alcohol suspends the fermentation and leaves the port sweet, strong, and perfect to pair with chocolate.

HYDROMETER: A glass tube with a weighted bulb that features a graduated scale on the body of the tube. You use it to help determine the potential percentage of alcohol in your beverage. A hydrometer measures the density, or specific gravity, of a liquid. Water has a specific gravity of 1.0. The more sugar you add to it, the denser it becomes and the greater its specific gravity. When yeast converts the sugar in a liquid to alcohol, the specific gravity returns to about 1.0.

IRISH MOSS: This is a seaweed that's added when boiling fermentables, as when making beer or mead. Toss in just a pinch per gallon, five or ten minutes before turning off the heat. It bonds to proteins and other particles and drops them to the bottom of the pot.

ISINGLASS: A fining agent that removes protein, yeast particles, and tannins. Since it removes yeast, add it after the fermentation has ended. It doesn't clear cloudy beverages very well, so it's normally used to add a final polish, especially to light-colored beverages.

Strong Waters

LACTOSE: A milk sugar that adds sweetness and body to beverages. Since yeast can't convert lactose, it's a good addition to a beverage you are carbonating and want to sweeten. Note that some people are lactose intolerant and, like yeast, can't digest the sugar.

LEES: The solids that drop to the bottom of your fermentation vessel when you are making wine, primarily composed of yeast and proteins. If you were making beer, you would call it *trub*.

MALOLACTIC FERMENTATION: A process where an alcohol-tolerant bacteria converts crisp malic acid in a beverage into softer lactic acids, usually after the secondary fermentation has completed. Some beverages benefit from the conversion, and others do not. You can buy and add the bacteria to help ensure it will happen in your beverage or add sulfites to prevent it.

MALT: This is a grain, normally barley, that is sprouted so the starches in the grain will convert to sugars. When the conversion has reached its peak, the grain is toasted which stops the sprouting process and caramelizes the sugars. Malt is used to make beer and is available in grain form, or extracted into powder or syrup.

MALT SYRUP: Also known as malt extract, this thick syrup is simple to use when making beer. Syrups are available to make most types of beer and can include hop flavoring.

MEAD: An alcoholic beverage made by the fermentation of honey and water. Many ingredients can be added to the basic recipe.

MELOMEL: A mead with fruit or fruit juices added.

METHEGLIN: A mead with herbs and spices added.

MUST: Fruit juice in the process of becoming wine. Also, when making a mead, must is the honey and water mixture.

PECTIN ENZYME: Pectin enzymes break up pectins or help prevent them from linking together so a beverage clears more easily. Added at 1 teaspoon per gallon to room temperature, not hot, liquid.

PECTINS: Large carbohydrate molecules that don't clear properly in fermented beverages and can cause haziness. They're critical in jam and jelly making but annoying and undesirable in winemaking.

PORT: A fortified beverage made by adding grape brandy to partially fermented wine.

PRIMARY FERMENTATION: The stage during which most fermentation takes place, usually in a covered widemouthed vessel.

PYMENT: Honey and grape juice fermented together. Pyment can also include spices.

RACKING: The careful transfer of a beverage from one container to another so that only the clear liquid is dispensed. The sediment, along with a small amount of beverage, remains in the first container. Racking is often accomplished by siphoning the beverage.

RACKING CANE: A stiff J-shaped plastic tube that makes siphoning the liquid out of a fermentation container much easier. A cap on one end elevates the bottom of the tube above the gunk at the bottom of the fermenter. The siphon hose attaches to the other end of the cane.

SECONDARY FERMENTATION: The stage at which fermentation finishes, normally in a glass carboy for beverages with higher alcohol levels such as wines and meads. For low-alcohol beverages, such as beer and cider, the fermentation finishes quickly enough that beverages don't need to be moved into a carboy. Secondary fermentation also includes the phase when a beverage passes through malolactic fermentation.

SORBATE (POTASSIUM SORBATE): An ingredient that helps prevent fermentation from restarting. Normally you use a sulfite to stop fermentation and then sorbate to help prevent refermentation and oxidizing. Adds a slight acidic taste.

Strong Waters

SPARKOLLOID: One teaspoon of this name-brand product dissolved in a little boiling water clears a gallon of fermented beverage. It has very little impact on flavor or color and compacts the lees on the bottom of the fermenter to make siphoning more efficient.

SPECIFIC GRAVITY: The reading taken from a hydrometer, which measures the density of fermentable liquid relative to water. Water has a specific gravity of 1.0. The more sugar you add to it, the denser it becomes and the greater its specific gravity. When yeast converts the sugar in a liquid to alcohol, the specific gravity returns to about 1.0.

STABILIZE: You stabilize a beverage by preventing it from further fermentation. The most common way to do this is to add a sulfite, such as potassium metabisulfite, which stops the yeast from converting any more sugars, and then add potassium sorbate, which prevents yeast from reproducing. Sulfite also helps prevent bacterial contaminations and loss of color.

STUCK FERMENTATION: When fermentation has stopped before the yeast has consumed all of the sugar, it is stuck. This can have several causes: the temperature is too high or low; the acid level is too high or low; there are not enough nutrients; the alcohol level is too high; there's too much sugar; or there's bacterial contamination. The first step to restarting a stuck fermentation is to compare your notes to the recipe. Using a yeast nutrient, an acid blend, or a less particular yeast will often restart a stuck fermentation.

SULFITE: Shorthand for sodium metabisulfite or potassium metabisulfite; used to stop yeast from fermenting. It can be added to fresh fruit before fermentation to kill off the wild yeast that nature added and at the end of fermentation to kill off the domestic yeast you added. Sulfite also helps stabilize the color in a beverage.

TANNIN: Found in fruit skins and stems, this compound adds astringency, helps protect a beverage from contamination, and helps prevent color change. Tannin can easily be added to fermentable liquids by using powdered grape tannin or toasted oak sawdust, both of which are available from home winemaking supply stores.

TRUB: The solids that drop to the bottom of your fermentation vessel when you are making beer, primarily yeast and proteins. If making wine, it is called *lees*.

WINE: The fermented juice of fruits with an alcohol content of 8 percent to 20 percent. Beverages of less than 8 percent are often considered ciders; wine seldom gets to more than 20 percent unless it's fortified with distilled spirits.

WINE THIEF: A glass tube with a hole on either end used to take a sample of a beverage that's either fermenting or aging. You place the tube beneath the surface of the wine and cover the other hole with your thumb, which creates a vacuum, allowing you to remove the sample.

WORT: Unfermented beer.

YEAST: Yeast is a single-celled fungus that converts sugar to alcohol and carbon dioxide. While there are hundreds of varieties of wild yeast floating around, people making fermented beverages select from a few dozen domesticated varieties.

YEAST ENERGIZER, OR YEAST NUTRIENT: A powdered nutrient containing vitamins and trace elements that is added to liquids to give yeast what they need to ferment. Use the kind that is made from yeast hulls and add ½ teaspoon per gallon.

Sizes and Conversions

WHEN MAKING A new recipe, use a hydrometer to determine the final alcohol level. If you find the level will be too low, add some fermentable sugar. Adding 1 cup of white sugar per 1 gallon of beverage will increase the potential alcohol level by 3 percent. (For example, if you had 2 gallons of beverage and the hydrometer reading was 9 percent, you could add 2 cups of white sugar to raise the final alcohol level to 12 percent.) If using a different sugar source, consult the charts below for the amount that will achieve the same 3 percent increase.

THIS VOLUME	EQUALS THIS WEIGHT	WHICH YIELDS THIS
1 cup of sugar	8 ounces	3% alcohol per gallon
2 cups of raisins	12 ounces	3% alcohol per gallon
2/3 cups of honey	10 ounces	3% alcohol per gallon
2/3 cups of malt	11 ounces	3% alcohol per gallon

SOME COMMON VOLUME CONVERSIONS

1 U.S. gallon	= 128 ounces	= 4.8 standard wine bottles (450 ml)	
1 U.S. gallon	= 4 quarts	= 8 pints	= 16 cups
1 U.S. quart	= 2 pints	= 4 cups	= 32 ounces
1 U.S. cup	= 8 ounces	= 16 tablespoons	= 48 teaspoons
4 tablespoons	= ¼ cup		
3 teaspoons	= 1 tablespoon		

Pearson's Square

WHEN BLENDING BEVERAGES, especially those with significantly different percentages of alcohol, you probably have a target alcohol strength for the final result in mind. This is especially true when making port, which is made by adding brandy to a batch of partially fermented wine to achieve a 20 percent alcohol content. The additional alcohol from the brandy stops the yeast from further fermenting the wine. The technique of adding a distilled spirit to a fermenting beverage can be used for more than just wine. But how does this work?

Say you have a quart of 8 percent wine and a brandy that's 40 percent alcohol, and you want to end up with 20 percent port. How much brandy should you add to the quart of wine?

The easiest way to figure this out is by using a technique called Pearson's Square.

In the illustration below:

A is the percentage of alcohol in your wine.
B is the amount of wine.
C is the percentage of alcohol in your spirit.
D is the amount of spirit.
X is the percentage of alcohol you want your fortified wine to be.
C – X = B
X – A = D
D/B is the proportion of spirit to wine in the final mixture.

Strong Waters

A		B
	X	
C		D

So for our example,

C − X = B or 40 − 20 = 20

X − A = D or 20 − 8 = 12

8		20
	20	
40		12

So for every 20 units of wine, you would need 12 of brandy: in other words a ratio of 12 to 20, which is .6. So if you have a quart of wine (32 ounces), you would need 19 ounces of brandy: 32 x .6 = 19

If this is more math than you want to bother with, there are Web sites that do the conversion for you. For example, Jack Keller's winemaking site has one: http://winemaking.jackkeller.net/blending.asp

Other Sources of Information

THERE'S A WEB SITE for this book: www.strongwaters.net. Feel free to email recipes, questions, and feedback.

Here are some other resources that I think you'll find helpful in making beverages.

Berry, C. J. J. *First Steps in Winemaking*. Ann Arbor, MI: G. W. Kent, 1995. Over 150 recipes in this 1980s volume show that you can make wine out of just about any plant.

Brew Your Own magazine. Battenkill Communications, Manchester Center, VT. www.byo.com. You can order a free copy of this magazine, aimed at amateur home brewers, from the Web site, and also access articles from previous issues, recipes, and resources such as a chart of yeast strains.

Buhner, Stephen Harrod. *Sacred and Herbal Healing Beers: The Secrets of Ancient Fermentation*. Boulder, CO: Siris Books, 1998. If you're searching for inspiration to break you out of making clone beers, read this book and realize there is an untapped world beyond malt and hops.

Crowe, Alison. *The Wine Maker's Answer Book*. North Adams, MA: Storey Publishing, 2007. This technical but approachable guide answers every question you'll have on making wine.

Digby, Kenelm. *The Closet of Sir Kenelm Digby Knight Opened*, edited, with introduction, notes, and glossary, by Anne Macdonell. London: Philip Lee Warner, 1910. Most books that refer to old recipes give a humble bow to this classic compendium. Granted, some of the recipes refer to quantities such as the hogshead, which, unless you repurpose your water heater, are impractical at home. Still, it offers good recipes to play with. After centuries of waiting, it's now blessedly available for a free download here: www.gutenberg.org/etext/16441.

Garey, Terry. *The Joy of Home Winemaking*. New York: Avon Books, 1996. This handy guide to winemaking includes a lot of tips, in addition to dozens of recipes.

Gayre, Robert. *Brewing Mead: Wassail! In Mazers of Mead*. Boulder, CO: Brewers Publications, 1986. Fascinating history of what for centuries was the most revered beverage in Western civilization. The 1986 edition has a helpful section by Charlie Papazain on brewing mead.

Grieve, Maude. *A Modern Herbal*. New York: Dover Publications, 1971. The definitive compendium of what was known about herbs before the twentieth century. Now available online: www.botanical.com/botanical/mgmh/mgmh.html.

Katz, Ellix Sandor. *Wild Fermentation: The Flavor, Nutrition, and Craft of Live-Culture Foods*. White River Junction, VT: Chelsea Green Publishing, 2003. If you're interested in fermented beverages as living foods, take the next step and read this inspirational and broader treatment of all things fermented—even goat.

Keller, Jack. *Winemaking Home Page: For the Beginner, Novice, and Seasoned Hobbyist*. http://winemaking.jackkeller.net. When you look for recipes online, it won't be long before you run into this Web site. One of the oldest wine recipe sites, it's broken and hard to navigate but full of recipes and solid procedures. It's a great site to start with, since it includes links to most of the other sites you'll need to make wine or meads.

McGee, Harold. *On Food and Cooking: The Science and Lore of the Kitchen*. New York: Scribner, 2004. The best book ever written for learning what happens as you prepare anything to drink or eat. While there's only one chapter on wine, beer, and distilled spirits, lifetimes of learning are distilled into its sixty-some pages.

Murry, Michael T., Joseph Pizzorno, and Laura Pizzorno. *The Condensed Encyclopedia of Healing Foods*. New York: Atria Books, 2005. Great reference book if you're interested in making beverages that are good for you.

Papazian, Charlie. *The New Complete Joy of Home Brewing*. New York: Avon Books, 1984. If you want to try all-grain brewing rather than the malt syrup recipes in this book, start here.

Pollan, Michael. *The Botany of Desire: A Plant's-Eye View of the World*. New York: Random House, 2001. Admittedly, this isn't a book on fermented beverages; the premise is to experience the world from the perspective of plants, and taking that viewpoint will enhance your appreciation of ingredients and how yeast works with them.

Renfrow, Cindy. *A Sip Through Time: A Collection of Old Brewing Recipes*. Self-published, 1997. Lots of classic recipes to explore here; making "cock ale" out of a rooster is high on my to-do list. Seriously, this volume has hundreds of recipes for beverages that people have enjoyed for generations and that aren't made anymore. Mine it for your own treasures.

WineMaker magazine. Battenkill Communications, Manchester Center, VT. www.winemakermag.com. You can order a free copy of this magazine aimed at amateur winemakers from their Web site, and also access articles from previous issues. The site has other resources as well, such as a chart of yeast strains that explains what beverages each strain makes, the temperature at which it works best, and its alcohol tolerance.

Zymurgy magazine. Brewers Association, Boulder, CO. www.beertown.org/homebrewing/zymurgy_magazine/index.html. This magazine is aimed at homebrewers and commercial craft brewers. It has a good index of recipes.

Acknowledgments

I AM AN inspired, motivated, and obsessed amateur who is continually astounded, not by my own efforts, or even by those who have handed down recipes and ingredients to us, but by what William Blake referred to as "the Genius of our world." I do not profess to be an expert in making the recipes in this book. Often the best we can do in life is prepare, hope for great results, and take what comes with good humor. This is certainly true when making fermented beverages. Choose the best ingredients and be careful with your preparation; once you add the yeast, it's mostly out of your hands. People may praise your prowess when they taste the results, but the longer I am at this business, the more I understand how much of the credit is beyond the execution of a recipe. So, much thanks to the Genius—and I certainly don't mean mine.

That said, this text involved the efforts of many people. I am completely indebted to everyone who has preceded me with recipes, ingredients, passions, and procedures. Some of the culprits are listed in the section "Other Sources of Information." My best hope for this book is that you—yes, I'm talking to you right now—will use this and similar books as a way to better connect to the Genius of the world.

Also particularly, though in no particular order, thanks to these people who have helped bring you this book: Robin Rinaldi for love, support, edits, ideas, and the patience that goes with living for many years in apartments and houses full of fermenting liquids; Frankie Frankeny for guidance and gorgeous photos; Antonio Sindorf for his fantastic illustrations; Sue Ducharme for her careful edits; Matthew Lore at The Experiment, my publisher, for propelling me through the process of getting this book published; Jasmine Star for performing the literary root planing and curettage that this book needed to sport a healthy smile; Karen Giangreco for her kind, organized, and persistent work in putting the pieces together; the San Francisco Writers Workshop for coherent criticism; Griz and the rest of the staff at San Francisco Brewcraft for answers and suggestions; the staff at Keystone Homebrew in Montgomery, Pennsylvania, for early encouragement and help; Kari Flores at Crazy Flower Farm in Napa, California, for answers to questions I didn't know to ask; Dave Pratt at dkcellars for commonsense suggestions on winemaking; Al Gore for helping bring us the Internet; Mike Yeater, Herb Radley, Tom Olson, and Earl Brown for recipe suggestions and a lifetime of support; and my parents for their love, encouragement, and example.

Index

[camera icon] indicates that the recipe is pictured in the photo insert.